Antonio Micallef

**Lectures on the Statutes of the Sacred Order
of St. John of Jerusalem**
at the University (of Studies) of Malta 1792

Juris Fontes
Rechtsquellen in Vergangenheit und Gegenwart
Band 2

Herausgegeben von
Diemut Majer, Wolfgang Höhne und Wolf-Dieter Barz

Lectures on the Statutes of the Sacred Order of St. John of Jerusalem

at the University (of Studies) of Malta 1792

by
Antonio Micallef

translated from the original Italian
by
Michael Galea

with an introduction and appendices
edited by
Wolf-Dieter Barz and Michael Galea

 Scientific Publishing

original title:
„Lezioni su gli statuti del Sagr' Ordine Gerosolimitano nell' Università degli Studi di Malta"

Impressum

Karlsruher Institut für Technologie (KIT)
KIT Scientific Publishing
Straße am Forum 2
D-76131 Karlsruhe
www.ksp.kit.edu

KIT – Universität des Landes Baden-Württemberg und
nationales Forschungszentrum in der Helmholtz-Gemeinschaft

KIT Scientific Publishing 2012
Print on Demand

ISSN 1868-3576
ISBN 978-3-86644-402-7

Vorwort zur Schriftenreihe

JURIS FONTES, eine neue Schriftenreihe zur Rechtsgeschichte – ist das sinnvoll?

Diese Frage muss sich die Rechtsgeschichte stets stellen lassen, da Versuche, vertiefte rechtshistorische Kenntnisse für die tägliche, praktische juristische Arbeit als *Conditio-sine-qua-non* zu reklamieren oft wenig überzeugen. Also, ein Verzicht auf Rechtsgeschichte ohne nennenswerten Verlust? Denkt man an Einsteins Worte „Der Unterschied zwischen Vergangenheit, Gegenwart und Zukunft ist eine Illusion", so möchte man die Frage bejahen. Da die Juristerei jedoch nicht in einer heute lediglich errechenbaren Zeitwelt betrieben wird, ist sie an unsere real erfahrbare tägliche Welt von Vergangenheit, Gegenwart und Zukunft gebunden. So ist hier der Satz Peter Tremaynes, i.e. Peter Berresford Ellis, zutreffender: „Wenn wir die Vergangenheit nicht kennen, können wir die Gegenwart nicht verstehen und wenn wir die Gegenwart nicht verstehen, können wir keine bessere Zukunft schaffen" (aus: Tod in der Königsburg). Aus diesem Grunde ist die Beschäftigung mit der Rechtsgeschichte nicht nur persönlich erfüllend, nicht nur *l'art pour l'art*, sondern hat ihre allgemeine Berechtigung, selbst wenn sie in aller Regel nicht zur alltäglichen Fallbearbeitung notwendig ist.

JURIS FONTES, die Rechtsquellen, sind Anliegen dieser neuen Schriftenreihe. Darunter sollen aber keineswegs nur Texteditionen historischer Rechtsquellen fallen, sondern gleichermaßen Betrachtungen zu Rechtsquellen in der Reihe Aufnahme finden. Die Reihenherausgeber würden sich durchaus wünschen, dass darüber hinaus auch Sekundärquellen in dem Mittelpunkt einzelner Werke der Reihe stehen, so sie dann für die jeweils angesprochenen Rechtsfragen von grundlegender Bedeutung wurden und eventuell heute noch sind. Denn ein Brückenschlag von Vergangenheit zur Gegenwart ist ohnehin ein Anliegen der Reihenherausgeber.

Die Rechtsgeschichte ist sowohl eine juristische wie auch eine historische Hilfswissenschaft. Daher sind die Herausgeber froh, dass in ihrem Team beide Hauptdisziplinen vertreten sind, um so bei der Betreuung der Schriftenreihe ein möglichst weites Gesichtsfeld zu haben, wenn in Karlsruhe, der viel genannten *Residenz des Rechts*, ein Stück Rechtsgeschichte verortet werden soll.

In dieser stark verfassungsrechtlich geprägten Residenz ist es ein glücklicher Umstand, dass auch der zweite Band von Juris Fontes ein verfassungsrechtliches Thema aufgreift - die interne, historische Verfassung des Völkerrechtssubjektes *Malteserorden*, des frühneuzeitlichen maltesischen Landesherrn, mit seinen heute etwa 900 Jahre alten Verfassungsgrundsätzen. Zudem besteht zwischen Baden und Malta ein besonderer Bezug; war doch das sogenannte Johanniter- oder Malteserfürstentum Heitersheim, zwischen Freiburg und Basel gelegen, eine Art Zwillingsstaat Maltas. So nimmt es auch kaum wunder, dass eine Richterdelegation der modernen Ordensgerichte – heute mit Sitz in Rom – nach einem Besuch in Heitersheim vor einigen Jahren auch Gast des Bundesverfassungsgerichts und des Bundesgerichtshofs war.

Die Herausgeber würden sich sehr freuen, wenn die Schriftenreihe bei den Rechtshistorikern, aber auch bei allen anderen, an der Materie Interessierten, wohlwollend aufgenommen würde und sich in der Leserschaft auch Autoren beziehungsweise Herausgeber einzelner zukünftiger Werke in der Reihe fänden.

Karlsruhe, im Herbst 2012

Diemut Majer   *Wolfgang Höhne*   *Wolf-Dieter Barz*

Prologue for the new series *Juris Fontes*

A new series on the history of law – does this make sense?

This is a question which is often posed with reference to the history of law because the attempts to lay claim to in-depth knowledge on the history of law for the daily, practical juristic work as a *conditio-sine-qua-non* often failed to be convincing.

So is there an abdication from the history of law without a relevant loss? Just to mention Einstein. He said: "The difference between the past, the present and the future is an illusion." One would like to answer the question in the affirmative. However, since jurisprudence is practised in an ascertainable world of time, it is bound to our daily world of the past, the present and the future which is real and can be experienced. Thus in this case Peter Tremayne's, alias Peter Berresford Elli's quotation is more applicable: "If we do not know the past, we are not able to understand the present and if we do not understand the present we are not able to create a better future" from his book *The Monk Who Vanished*. For this reason the preoccupation with the history of law is not only individually fulfilling, not only *l'art pour l'art*, but has a general right to exist, even if normally it is not essential to the common handling of law cases.

Juris Fontes, the sources of law, are the subject matter of this new series. Yet the series is not only supposed to contain editions of historical sources of law but reflections on these sources of law shall be likewise reviewed. In addition the editors of the series would wish to place special emphasis on secondary sources which are the pivotal element of some works of the series in that they became more important to the questions of law mentioned specifically and are eventually of significance even today. Anyhow, bridge building between the past and the present is one of the editors' concerns.

The history of law is a legal as well as a historical ancillary science. Therefore, the editors are glad that both main disciplines are involved in their team so that they have a broad field of vision while working with the series. In Karlsruhe, the oftentimes mentioned *Residenz des Rechts*, one piece of the history of law is supposed to be located. Here in fact the concentration of courts right up to the Federal Court of Justice and the Federal Constitutional Court is extra high; the city therefore is called the *residence of law*.

It is a happy occasion that in this residence characterized by constitutional law, the second publication of *Juris Fontes* takes up again a topic of constitutional law - the internal and historical constitution of the Order of Malta, a subject of public international law and an early modern Maltese territorial lord with its more than 900-year old constitutional principles. Furthermore there is a special connection between Baden in Germany and Malta because Heitersheim, the so-called Knights of St. John's principality (or the principality of the Order of Malta) located between Basel and Freiburg, was somehow a twin state of Malta. So it is no wonder that a few years ago a delegation of judges from the modern courts of the Order – today based in Rome – were also guests of the Federal Constitutional Court and of the Federal Court of Justice after a visit in Heitersheim.

The editors would be very pleased if the series was appreciated by legal historians as well as by everyone who is interested in the subject matter. Authors or editors of similar works among our readers are welcome.

Karlsruhe, autumn 2012

Diemut Majer   *Wolfgang Höhne*   *Wolf-Dieter Barz*

Prologue translated by Jaqueline Beck

CONTENTS

PART I

PART II

PART III

Constitutional Charter and Code of the Sovereign
Military Hospitaller Order of St. John of Jerusalem,
of Rhodes and Malta [1998]

PART I

Introduction

It is thought that Antonio Micallef's *Lezioni su gli statuti del Sagr' Ordine Gerosolimitano nell' Università degli Studi di Malta* (Lectures on the Statutes of the Sacred Order of St. John of Jerusalem at the University of Studies of Malta) compiled in 1792 should be edited here in an English version. This work deals with lectures which Micallef himself delivered at the University of the Sovereign Military Order of St. John in its State of Malta at the late baroque period.

The idea of a new edition of Micallef's work is suggested for two reasons: it provides a study of the (legal) history of the Order and of the University of Malta.

To conform with the aim of this series of publications, that is, history, past and present, it would be expedient to give an outline of the Order's history and of the University. A short biographical note about professor Antonio Micallef is included. Through him we acquaint ourselves with sources concerning the legal structure of the Order obtaining in Malta at the end of the eighteenth century. To bridge the past with the present the Order's Constitution and Code which have come into force in recent years are reproduced as appendices. In this context thanks are due to the German Association of the Order who has courteously provided the officially translated English text of the *Carta Costituzionale* (Constitutional Charter) and the *Codice* (Code). (In addition the official version of the English text which has been in the meantime published by the Order in the United Kingdom, has been also consulted <http://www.orderofmalta .org.uk/downloads/Constitution_Charter_and_code.pdf>). By means of a possible comparison the reader can better understand the passage leading from past to the modern legal environment of the Order. Thereby the reader also experiences for himself the exciting development of a *persona moralis* (here: a legal entity under Public International Law and Canon Law comprised of individuals) ruling a country to a *persona moralis* without any territorial identity but nevertheless assured of recognition in terms of Public International Law. Consequently, the various conditions are reflected in legal structure of the Order's past and present.

Hellwald mentions in his bibliography on the Order of Malta two historical standard, and perhaps most interesting, textbooks on the statutes of the Order[1]. One is compiled by the erstwhile Court President of the Maltese Supreme Court, Frà Christian von Osterhausen, in the year 1644[2], who addressed himself in particular to his younger German speaking Brethren, so that they could acquaint themselves with the *Statuta Ordnungen und Gebraeuche(n)* (Statutes, Ordinances and Customs) of their otherwise Italian speaking Order.

The second textbook i.e. *Lezioni su gli statuti* of the Order is published in 1791/92, and is likewise the work of an expert hand. The author of the latter work is the Maltese Frà Antonio Micallef, who was a chaplain of the Langue of Italy in the Order's Convent (Order's headquarters). The Order then consisted of eight Langues or Nationalities. He lectured at the University of Malta which was in its beginnings. He was primarily professor of Civil Law, but he also made a name as academical and scholarly lecturer on Law concerning the Order, which laid down to a certain extent the legal structure of the country. The publication of Micallef's *Lezioni* was to fulfil mainly the need to avoid for his students the dictation and transcription of his lectures. Moreover, the *Lezioni* were useful to whosoever had to study the Order's legal set-up. This was more significant as the statutes of the Order had been drafted afresh at the time of Prince Grandmaster Emanuel de Rohan Polduc (1775-1797). Today these regulations are still known as *Code Rohan* or *Codice di Rohan* after the Grandmaster[3]. The *Codice di Rohan* is still valid as a subsidiary source to the *Carta Costituzionale* and *Codice* now *in vigore* since 1998. As

---

[1] **Hellwald, [Ferdinand de]**: *Bibliographie méthodique...* 232.

[2] **Osterhausen, Christian von**: *Statuta, Ordnungen und Gebraeuche deß Hochlöblichen Ritterlichen Ordens S. Johannis von Jerusalem zu Malta,* Frankfurt a.M. 1644; (new print in **Barz, Wolf-Dieter**: *Das Wesen des Malteserordens und die Person des Christian von Osterhausen, eine Einführung für das Lehrbuch Osterhausens von 1644 zum Recht dieses Ordens,* Münster 1995.

[3] Codice del Sacro Militare Ordine Gerosolimitano, Malta 1782.

Micallef's *Lezioni* followed the *Codice di Rohan*, they help us indirectly, one may say, to better understand the present subsidiary element of the legal government of the Order. Thereby the present *Carta Costituzionale* and *Codice* become more intelligible. Moreover, the new edition of Micallef's *Lezioni* will revive the history of the University of Malta, which was the supreme academical institution of the Order and of the country.

The *Lezioni* were printed in limited number so that outside Malta Micallef's work is considered an extreme rarity even perhaps in well established and leading libraries. According to a hand-written catalogue of the National Library of Malta, Valletta, a further impression with almost identical text appeared one year before. Autoptically i.e. regarding the book itself, this cannot be proofed any more because the title-page of the first edition was replaced by photocopy of that of the second edition. Interestingly enough both books were printed in Malta *nella Stamp[eria] del Palazzo di S[ua] A[ltezza] E[minentissima] presso Fr[à] G[iovanni] M[allia]*, that is at the official printing press of the Order. The fact that the *Lezioni* were printed in the Order's printing press seems to give Micallef's work more weight and an implicit recognition of its importance. One should mention in this context that books, as well as legal texts, often were either hand-written or had to be sent to Italy for printing. The Press Law and the Liberty of the Press in Malta was an extremely complicated matter. Although he was the lord of the country, the Grand Master had limited power as regards the press because of jurisdictional reasons and censorship, with which the Bishop and the Roman Inquisitor were also invested.

In the National Library of Malta there is an elegant manuscript consisting of about 40 folios written and signed by Antonio Micallef himself; it directly concerns the *Lezioni*. This *memoriale* (document) entitled *Commento dei Statuti del Sac(ro) Ordine Gerosol(limita)no* contains a synopsis and an abridged form of the *Lezioni* and is addressed to the *Altezza Emminentissima*, that is, to Grandmaster Rohan, whereby Micallef requests the authorization enabling him to print his work[4].

---

[4] National Library of Malta, MS. 489.

COMMENTO DEI STATUTI DEL SAC. ORDINE GEROSOL.no

Alterza Eminentissima

Mi do l'onore di presentare all'
Alterza Vostra il principio del mio
Commento sul Codice di questo Sacro
Ordine, perche si degni giudicare, se il
mio impegno è di qualche fatica. Badi,
che se per lavoro, o buono, o cattivo che sia,
lo riconoscerà, allora la sua Giustizia che
lo rende adorabile a tutti li suoi Religiosi,
e Vassalli, l'obbligherà alla conseguenza.
Intanto pieno di vero ossequio mi do l'altro
onore di ratificarmi
Di V. A. Ema

fra Antonio Micallef

An ad hoc Commission was set up to examine and report on Micallef's work, following his request to print the *lezioni*. Permission was subsequently granted but the Commission made it emphatically clear that the *lezioni* should not and could not be taken as interpreting the Statutes and Ordinances of the Order in any of its Tribunals in order to safeguard and ensure their absolute and complete independence from academical research and teaching.

Micallef was writing particularly to students in Malta and to the Order itself; both were widely conversant with the Italian language. By way of contrast, today only part of the Order's members understands Italian, and in Malta itself the country's own language and the widespread knowledge of English have pushed Italian in the background. This edition of the *Lezioni* merits being made available to a much wider readership, and is, therefore, being presented in English.

It may not be amiss to mention that Micallef's standard textbook in use in the old Faculty of law was exhibited as a rare item in the Aula Magna of the former University building in Valletta in November 1992, marking the Quatercentenary (1592-1992) of the *Collegium Melitense* (u/m).

In 1999 the Order celebrated the Ninth Centenary of its foundation. However, little is generally known about the Order itself. This applies in particular as regards its legal system and even its development in general, although in rudimental sections not too much has changed since the Middle Ages: The Order is today the last active Order of Chivalry having a canonical character in the tradition of its concept foundation.

A brief history of the Order of St. John

The status of the Order as subject of Public International Law and its Constitution and Statutes can be better understood with an historical background. According to Art. 1 of its Constitution the official name of the Order is *Sovrano Militare Ordine Ospedaliero di San Giovanni di Gerusalemme, detto di Rodi, detto di Malta* (Sovereign Military Hospitaller Order of St. John of Jerusalem, of Rhodes, and of Malta), which readily denotes its international character and history.

In 1048 merchants from Amalfi, southern Italy, set up a hospice and a hospital community in Jerusalem. They brought with them the eight-pointed cross, the emblem of Amalfi, today commonly known as Maltese Cross. With the conquest of Jerusalem from the 'Infidels' at the time of the First Crusade in 1099 the brethren started running their newly-built and large hospital. The brethren could nurse the numerous wounded knights and soldiers in the Holy Land; they became hospitallers in the proper sense of the word. This was reason enough for the Order of the Hospitallers to commemorate in 1999 their nine hundred years of service to "Our Lords the sick and poor".

Up to 1154 this community developed gradually into an Order, which was named after John the Baptist, as its Patron and Protector. The members of the Order were bound by the vows of Chastity, Poverty and Obedience, and from 1118 onwards they also made the vow to fight the Muslims. Thereby the Order merged in the military movement of the crusades. In spite of its military tasks the Order did not lose its charitable activity. The development to an international and noble military Order as a powerful regional factor, and similarly to a sovereign position together with an internal secularisation became more evident. Through pious foundations, bequests, donations and acquisitions it accumulated considerable immovable land property in several Christian countries. The will to rule, military power, possession of land and people, the many privileges, numerous royalties gave the Order an initial impetus and position as territorial ruler in the Near East. The development process, however, failed again and again during the warring entanglement of the crusades. But then the Order obtained as fief in a definite form by atypical agreements (e.g. no compulsory military duties) under feudal law, territories in the Principality of Antiochia and in the Earldom Tripoli. In virtue of these agreements the Order acted as if it were sovereign over these territories; in practice this meant, for example, that it could on its own initiative make war against the Muslim rulers.

As a historical anticipation it would be mentioned here that also priories, bailiwicks and commanderies of the provinces of the Order in Europe sometimes attained state legal rights. Thus in the bailiwick of Miravet in the Kingdom of Aragon, the Order had legislative power over the inhabitants of Miravet who in this aspect were not subject to the King but to the Grandmaster, Head of the Order [5], whereas in Germany the Grand Prior, being an Imperial Prince ruled with legislative power over Heitersheim and its adjacent territories[6]. Moreover, there had been jurisdictional privileges.

The last defended fortress of the crusade States, Jean d'Acre, fell in Muslim hands in 1291. From there seven surviving knights fled to the Latin Kingdom of Cyprus, where they established anew the Order's convent. There the Order came under the feudal dependence of the King of Cyprus-Jerusalem of the dynasty of the Lusignans; the knights had to carry out military duty for the monarch, and as a result of which they lost their independence.

For the re-acquisition of its independence, the Order conquered Rhodes from 1304 onwards, and finally the whole Dodecannes. With the city of Rhodes as its centre, the Order established itself as Christian bridgehead within seeing distance of the growing Ottoman Empire. By 1310 the political situation was safe enough for the Order to enable it to transfer its seat from Limassol in Cyprus to the city of Rhodes. Here the Order introduced its federal structures of eight Langues which became known after the countries or regions of the knights' origin. In altered form the many National Associations constitute nowadays the Order's

---

[5] **Sanchez, Galo** (ed): *Constituciones Baiulie Mirateti*, Madrid 1915.
[6] **Barz, Wolf-Dieter (ed)**: *Die Heitersheimer Herrschaftsortdnung des Johanniter-/Malteserordens von 1620*, Münster 1999.

branches. The former Langues extended from Poland in the East up to England in the West, from Scandinavia in the North as far as Spain and Sicily in the South. Thus the Order already functioned in anticipation to the European Union: it embodied and embraced an all-European concept. It showed common European interests by policing and protecting from Muslim pirates or Turkish raids and molestation cargo and merchandise ships from Europe. Indeed, it traced back its identity from the European idea of *una civitas (christiana)*.

In 1382 the Bailiwick of Brandenburg of the Grand-Priory of Germany signed an agreement in Heimbach, whereby the Bailiwick enhanced its autonomy. In the wake of the Lutheran Reformation it became protestant, without dissolving itself completely from the Priory's union. The resultant status is difficult to define especially in terms of Canon Law. The Prussian King, at the same time *summus episcopus* in his Kingdom, dissolved the Bailiwick in 1811, but it was re-established by his successor in 1852. It is now generally known by the name *Johanniterorden*.

After the siege by the Turks and the ensuing occupation of Rhodes, the Order had to relinquish the city in the very beginning of the year 1523. The Order left the island with military honours together with a number of Rhodians; the knights carried with them the archives, which dated back to the times of the crusades (now jealously kept in the National Library of Malta). The extensive Archives of the Order in Malta contain 6524 manuscript volumes comprising records drawn up in the Holy Land, Cyprus, Rhodes, Rome and Malta over the years 1107 – 1798.

For the next seven years the Order wandered in the western region of the Mediterranean.

In 1530 Emperor Charles V, as Spanish monarch and ruler of the Kingdom of Sicily, handed over to the Order the Maltese Archipelago as fief, which pertained to Sicily. Although the island was given as fief no military service was imposed in favour of the feudal overlord. The Order became almost an independent ruler, and legally responsible for Malta and the African enclave of Tripoli. At the same time Malta became a bulwark against the advancing Turks, who in 1565 tried in vain to force their way across the island to the European mainland. After its new headquarters the Order is now more often known as Order of Malta.

On his campaign to Egypt in 1798 Napoleon conquered Malta and expelled the Order from the island.

As the Order has since become almost an anachronistic relic of the crusades in Europe, which had experienced the French Revolution, its existence was seriously threatened. Meanwhile, some members of the Order sought the protection of the Russian Czar Paul I, who was particularly inclined to the chivalrous tradition. Subsequently he became *de facto* Grandmaster of the Order; the headquarters of the Convent was set up in St. Petersburg.

As the succeeding Czar did not want to continue the dignity of Grandmaster, the Order's headquarters moved to Italy in 1803. From 1834 onwards the government of the Order established its present headquarters in its former embassy in Rome in via Condotti; there the Order took up permanent residence with privileges of extraterritorial rights as a sovereign body in terms of Public International Law. The Order today embraces 12000 members all over the world.

The Order now dedicates itself exclusively to charitable and humanitarian activities within its own sovereignty. Its second seat of historical significance on parts of its former Fort St. Angelo in Malta (Birgu / Vittoriosa) is not a microstate, but a special territory by International Law under Maltese sovereignty. Attempts in seeking a new territory for the Order or a Trust have resumed in the recent past, but this is not an essential or deciding matter.

The fascinating consideration of the Order's legal history is its involvement as a constitutional unit in completely different legal spheres, namely the ecclesiastical, the Order's own sphere, the international and the national (wherever branches of the Order exist). More fascinating, however, is the fact that the Order as a constitutional unit has now existed for more than nine hundred years, during which its external conditions have often changed radically without changing basically the Order itself and its constitutional system. The Order is probably in this sense the most astonishing legal body in European culture circles, about which Antonio Micallef, more than two hundred years ago, based his lectures at the University in Malta – hence the printing of Micallef's work translated in English text.

Having dealt with the Order's history and its development, one should not omit mentioning the Order's University in Malta. It should be considered a great cultural achievement for a country with a population, in those days, of 130,000 inhabitants to have its own university. The Order, notwithstanding its noble and chivalrous, military and hospitaller, warring and medical character succeeded in founding an university, which is an eminently academical institution.

In this context *Waldstein-Wartenberg* in his work entitled *Die Vasallen Christi, Kulturgeschichte des Johanniterorden im Mittelalter* mentioned[7], that the Order did not only dedicate itself to fighting and caring the sick and poor but indulged in cultural activities; this is particularly interesting as he was writing about the Order in the Middle Ages. This is, indeed, an aspect of the Order's history which to date has not been sufficiently studied.

---

[7] **Waldstein-Wartenberg, Berthold:** *Die Vasallen Christi, Kulturgeschichte des Johanniterordens im Mittelalter,* Wien et alt. 1988.

The University of Malta - its Origin and Development

As the Order of St. John of Jerusalem took over the island in 1530, Malta started its way to independent Nationhood – even though it was under foreign domination. In 1964 this development attained full Independence under Public International Law having its own government. For such a very small country like Malta, its own scientific and cultural permanency seems to be of quite special significance to imagine itself as a Nation. Under the rule of the Order the political disentanglement from the spanish-sicilian connection was further pursued; this meant a step towards national independence. With the foundation of the University, Malta also owes to the Order its first step towards a modern and permanent development in the sciences.

The Portuguese Prince Grandmaster Manuel Pinto de Fonseca, who ruled the Order for more than 30 years – up till then the longest reign of a grandmaster (1741-1773) – was destined to leave a lasting mark in the Order. Known for his political haughtiness, prodigal administration and lifestyle, he was indeed a late baroque autocrat.

He was such a fascinating personality that in 1989 the Maltese historian Testa flattered him with a voluminous biography[8]. Pinto did not only introduce the Royal Crown in the Order's coat-of-arms, but, like many other baroque rulers, he promoted culture and science. He set a landmark in Malta's own cultural sphere by founding the *Publica Università di Studi Generali* (Public University) on November 22, 1769, which commenced functioning in 1771.

Amongst other professors Antonio Micallef was the first to occupy the chair of Civil Law, when he was 46, and continued to lecture on this subject up to 1809[9].

---

[8] **Testa, Carmel:** *The Life and times of Grand Master Pinto.*
[9] Micallef's contemporary professors were: 1: Sacred Scripture: P. Ferdinando Mingarelli, who also taught Aramaic and Greek; 2: Dogmatic Theology: P. Maestro (Francesco) Bonnici OFM Conv., who also taught Moral Theology; 3: Canon Law: P. Stanislao of Jesus, Discalced Carmelite; 4: Medicine: Dr. Giorgio Lucano, who also taught Botany: 5: Surgery: Dr. Michelangelo Grima, who also taught Anatomy and

Pinto succeeded in attracting to Malta numerous foreign professors for teaching and research, thereby raising the University to an international institution. It needs hardly be stressed that the Pope, who once had control over teaching institutions in Europe, readily gave his consent to the founding of the University by the Order in Malta, the more so as it concerned the faculty of Theology.

Without in any way diminishing Pinto's merits in founding the University, one must at this stage mention the two institutions which preceded it. For the University did not come into being out of nothing.

Of special significance is the *Collegium Melitense*, a school run by the Jesuits. Founded in 1592 it opened its doors a year later. In that same year Grandmaster Hugues Loubeux de Verdala (1582-1595) laid the foundation stone for a new building of the College in Valletta, the newly-built capital city of the Order in Malta. In 1594 the College was ready for use. Attendance in this school qualified for further study in any other University. Gradually the teaching of Theology played an increasing role. Hence it is not to be wondered at, that 1727 the General of the Jesuit Order assigned the Rector of the College the right to confer academical degrees. And the country's ruler, Grandmaster Anton Manoel de Vilhena (1722-1736) confirmed this right. In this manner a sort of theological-philosophical college was born. The Order of St. John promoted the Jesuit College in many ways, but did not attach to the College its own educational and cultural interest for the country. When the Jesuits had to leave Malta temporarily during the administration of Grandmaster Jean Paul de Lascaris Castellar (1636-1657), one did not want to re-open the College because, it was thought, there was more need of soldiers and seamen rather than of doctorates and academics, of whom Malta had more than enough to the detriment of the Principality.

Surgery; 6: Logica and Metaphysics: P. Angelo Moncada, Dominican, who also taught Natural Law; 7: Physics: P. Atanasius Cavalci, Carmelite, who also taught Moral Philosophy; 8: Mathematics: Abbate Fra Giovanni Alberico Archinto; 9: Rhetorics: Abbate Giuseppe Scerri; 10: Humanism: Abbate Braccelli; 11: Grammar: Fra Bruno and Fra Aquilina, both Dominicans; 12: Reading and Literature: Fra Matteo Gile and Fra Giuseppe Portelli, both Members of the Order of St. John.

Meanwhile there was another very active educational institution. On December 19, 1676, a school of Botany, Anatomy, Medicine and Surgery (originally it did not form part of Medicine) was incorporated in and attached to the major Hospital of the Order, the *Sacra Infermeria* (Holy Infirmary) in Valletta. Its founder Grandmaster Nicolas Cotoner (1663-1680) engaged the Maltese member of the Order, the Reverend Don Giuseppe Zammit, as the school's first lecturer. For centuries it now became a tradition to entrust the teaching of Medicine in Malta to local teachers. A moot point of this school were evidently the faculties of Anatomy and Surgery. Zammit set up in Fort St. Elmo, close to the Hospital in Valletta, a botanical garden, which was later removed to the suburb of Floriana, where it still exists. About its founder little is known. Tradition has it, Zammit bequeathed his voluminous library to the Order's Hospital. Together with the other books of the Hospital, these book collections were transferred in 1797 to the new public library, now the National Library of Malta.

Three more persons may be mentioned in connection with the School of Anatomy. From 1723 to 1753 Gabriele Henin taught in Malta. Under Grandmaster Marc' Antonio Zondadari (1720-1722) he was sent to the famous hospital of Santa Maria Nuova in Florence to study practical Anatomy. Grandmaster Vilhena recalled him to Malta, where Henin became father of modern Anatomy. He dissected human bodies, and in 1749 published in Messina his surgical-anatomical work entitled *Observatio chirurgo-anathomica*. Since the time of Zondadari – and this shows the open-mindedness of the Order – corpses of members of the Order and of those patients, who died in the Hospital, were placed at disposal for dissections.

From 1763 to 1797 Michelangelo Grima, a former pupil of Henin, was assigned the lectureship. Later on Pinto appointed him as first Maltese professor of Anatomy and Surgery. Under Grima, a graced practitioner and scientist – his legacy and his publications still exist – Malta experienced in its teaching faculties such an impetus, that it attracted foreign students. One of his pupils, who later on became famous, was the German-Maltese Giuseppe Barth, who, encouraged by the Order, in later years became professor of Anatomy and Ophthalmologist in Vienna, and as physician in the Imperial Court, an internationally recognized figure. As the only erstwhile Maltese student he taught Medicine in the German Empire. It would be noted that the Order was obviously open to the idea of women's instruction. Otherwise it is hard to explain that at its own expense in 1772 it even sent a young woman to Florence to study Surgery.

On the occasion of the 300th anniversary of the foundation of the School of Anatomy and Surgery, the Rector of the University recalled that Pinto merged this School with the Jesuit College to form the new University. This deed was preceded by the expulsion of the Jesuit Order from Malta. Following protracted negotiations Pinto succeeded in obtaining papal consent, so that the Jesuits' property in Malta became the Order's property. This move helped replenish in part the Order's precarious finances brought about by Pinto's lavish lifestyle. In this manner - not only in a financial sense – the basis for the new University was attained. The newly-founded University now moved into the old premises of the College in St. Paul Street in Valletta. Accommodation to the professors was also afforded in the same building.

Pinto himself stipulated and laid down the *Constituzioni per i nuovi Studj dell' Università e per il Collegio di Educazione di Malta* (university legislation) – manuscript document extant[10]. The teaching institution was strongly and firmly subject to the Order, as one would notice that the academical year ended on 24 June, being the feast-day of St. John the Baptist, Patron of the Order. Theology, Jurisprudence and Medicine must have constituted the three main faculties. Together with these faculties were also taught Mathematics, Literature, Botany and Chemistry. Attached to the University was a school of navigation, which, however, came under the Order's Admiral and the Congregation of the Galleys.

Following Pinto's death (1773) the finances of the Order were in such a precarious state, that the teaching institution in many instances had to be discontinued because it could not meet the expenses, and the foreign

---

[10] Archives of the Order (AOM), *Erectio Collegii et Universitatis Studiorum Melitensis,* Libr. Bullarum, MS. 253, f. 155.

professors had to return to their countries of origin. Pinto did not provide the University with its own source of revenue, so it rather had to meet expenditure from the common budget.

Soon the last significant Grandmaster in Malta, Rohan, revived the University. In 1776, after 145 years this skilful Grandmaster convened a Chapter General to work out anew the Order's statutes (*Codice del Sacro Militare Ordine Gerosolimitano, 1782*) and the Municipal legislation of the country (*Del Dritto Municipale di Malta, …, 1784*), and thus gave Malta a new comprehensive legal foundation, and for the last time strengthened the Order in its old tradition. However, the end of the Order as an Order of chivalry was already in the air. Whether Rohan was also thinking of the fate of the University remains uncertain. Hardly had Napoleon expelled the Order from Malta in 1798, the University had to close its doors.

However, already in 1800 the University could resume its teaching duties under the military command of Sir Alexander Ball, Civil Commissioner and Representative of the British Royal Crown. Gradually it grew, notwithstanding the many vicissitudes, to a modern University with the longest tradition in the British Colonial Empire.

In 1969 the University Campus in Msida, designed on modern architecture, was inaugurated. In 2007 the new University *Clinicum*, which is situated within the University complex, started functioning. The difficult times, brought about by a Socialist Government in 1970s, having receded, the University of Malta today runs the faculties of Medicine and Theology, both of which represent its mother faculties, once more under one roof. The University has about 10000 students; it confers Bachelorships, Masterships, Diplomas and Doctorates (Ph.D., M.D, LL.D.), the last mentioned are the most numerous. Thanks to the manifold international connections of the University these studies can be pursued also by foreigners.

The modern University of Malta is evidently in keeping with the tradition of its foundation by Grandmaster Pinto; this is explained by the University's own coat-of-arms, which portrays on two quarters the Order's white Cross on a red ground, and on two other quarters Pinto's personal arms, namely, five red crescents on a silver (white) field.

Commendatore Fra Antonio Micallef
1725 - 1809

Fra Antonio Micallef (Michallef) was born on 20 October 1725, when he was also baptized by the Parish Priest Father Joseph Cucciardi of the church of St. Paul Shipwecked of Valletta. His parents were Joseph and Maria spouses Michallef. The child was given the names: Dominic – Antonio – Xaver - Vincentio, but he was known by his second name: Antonio. The godparents at his christening were Joseph Azzupard, son of the late Dominic and Maria, wife of Joannis Moutepagani, both of Valletta [11]. Antonio was born at the time of the Portuguese Grandmaster Fra Anton Manoel de Vilhena (1723-1736).

Antonio studied for the priesthood. And after finishing his studies at the age of 28, he was received as Conventual Chaplain (or Priest of Obedience) in the Langue of Italy of the Hospitaller Order of St. John of Jerusalem on 8 October 1753 [12], at the time of the Portuguese Grandmaster Emanuel Pinto de Fonseca (1741-1773).

As Conventual Chaplain Fra Antonio Micallef served and officiated in the churches of the Order. His other duties included that of Almoner of the Holy Infirmary and that of accompaying the Order's navy on its sea voyages; the chaplains had papal permission to say Mass on the Order's galleys at sea. For this purpose very often folding and portable altars were used.

The house, where Fra Antonio Micallef must have lived in Valletta (at the corner of Merchants Street with Old Theatre Street) still stands. The house is known as Casa Bellott and was donated to the Assembly of Conventual Chaplains by Fra Carlo Bellott, senior. The Assembly of Conventual Chaplains demolished this house in 1745-47, and rebuilt it in the its present form [13]. The fact that Micallef's demise is recorded in the

---

[11] Parochial Archives St. Paul Shipwrecked Church, Valleta, Libr. Bapt. Vol. 11 (1705-1726), f. 510.

[12] MS Lista dei Cavalieri, Cappellani and Serventi d'Arme ricevuti nell'Ordine di S. Giovanni di Gerusalemme dal 1661 al 1797 [rollo], Vol. 1, f. 514, National Library of Malta, Valletta.

[13] Cabreo Assemblea Vol. IV, National library of Malta, Treas. B 295 f. 30v., **Denaro Victor F.**, *The Houses of Valletta*, Malta, 1967, 28.

archives of the parish church of Our Lady of Porto Salvo seems to confirm this opinion as Casa Bellott was within the parochial limits of the said parish.

Fra Antonio Micallef distinguished himself for his erudition and literary acumen, and in particular for his deep knowledge of the Statutes of the Order.

The French Grandmaster Emanuel de Rohan Polduc carried out legislative reforms by re-structuring and re-organizing the courts and revising the municipal laws. He entrusted the compilation of the new code to Giandonato Rogadeo, "a most distinguished lawyer" [14] from Bitonto, near Naples. Since Rogadeo advocated the retention of torture, one doubted how far-reaching his ideals for reform were. Being a stranger, Rogadeo did not acquaint himself with the nature, needs and customs of the people for whom he was compiling the code of laws. He soon fell foul of the local Maltese jurists and levelled charges against the Maltese in general and against members of the legal profession in particular. No wonder that the proposed code did not receive the approval of Maltese jurists nor of the special Commission appointed by Rohan.

Thirty-two months after his coming to Malta, Rogadeo returned to Naples – overwhelmed with sarcasm, bitterness, and an unquenchable lust to settle scores.

In 1780 Rogadeo published in Lucca, Italy, his *Ragionamenti sull'amministrazione della giustizia in Malta* – a diatribe against his adversaries of the legal profession and against the Maltese. Micallef was amongst those who replied to Rogadeo's work. In 1782 Micallef published also in Lucca his *Prospectus*, being a defence of the people of Malta against the accusations of Rogadeo [15].

---

[14] **Bonello, G.,** „How a stranger saw the Maltese Legal Profession in 1781" in *the Sunday Times* [of Malta], 13.12.1992.

[15] **Saydon, Pietru Pawl**, *List of Publications by Members of the Teaching Staff of the University* [of Malta], Malta, 1966, 30.

Subsequently the compilation proper of the new Municipal Code was entrusted to Federigo Gatto, a Maltese, ably aided by Commendatore Fra Antonio Micallef, and others [16].

Micallef has published several publications between 1758 and 1796 dealing generally with law cases; some publications were printed in Italy [17].

Fra Antonio Micallef was a professor of Civil Law in the University of Malta from 1771 up to his death (1809) with a brief interruption between 1798 and 1800, during the French occupation of the Island.

As a number of modest commanderies than those of the Knights were reserved for the chaplains [18], Commendatore Fra Antonio Micallef was assigned a commandery in one of the Priories of the Langue of Italy. The assignment of a commandery was always considered a sign of recognition and appreciation for services rendered; it also meant a fixed income and not unimportant social status.

Fra Antonio Micallef must have found special favour with the German Grandmaster Fra Ferdinand von Hompesch (1797-1798) for he wanted to express his gratitude by publishing an *Ode*, written in Italian in praise of Fra Ferdinand Hompesch on the occasion of the latter's election to the Headship of the Order [19]. This flattering work dedicated to the Grandmaster – a customary gesture in the baroque era – certainly did not impair Micallef's reputation and career. His proven literary and academic ability has contributed in no small measure to his outstanding distinction in the Order.

---

[16] „diede molto ajuto col suo lume" (cfr Malta National Library MS. 1142, no foliation)

[17] **Hellwald, Ferdinand de**, *Bibiographie méthodique* ..., mentions from 249 to 259 most of Micallef's works. Moreover Hellwald refers to *Dritto Municipale* (1784) promulgated by Grandmaster Rohan published with annotations by a certain Antonio Micallef in 1843, but in view of this date it would not seem probable or likely that the attribution to 'our' Micallef is correct. **Saydon**, 30; **Schembri, Antonio**, *Selva di Autori e Traduttori Maltesi*, Malta 1855, 50.

[18] **Sire, H(enry) J. A.**, *The Knights of Malta*, 83.

[19] *Ode dedicata a S[ua].A[ltezza]. S[erenissi]ma Fra Ferdinando Hompesch Gran Maestro di S[acro] O[rdine] [di] G[erusalemme]* ..., Malta (undated).

Commendatore Fra Antonio Micallef breathed his last on 24 May 1809, by which time Britain had established itself firmly on the island. Comforted by the rites of Holy Mother Church he peacefully passed away at the venerable age of 84[20] . He was laid to rest in the crypt beneath the Oratory of the church of St. John (also known as the crypt of Bartolott). No memorial epitaph marks his tomb. He was amongst the last members of the Order to be buried in the crypt of the church, after the Order had left the island.

Micallef lived through very eventful and turbulent years in Malta's history: the last decades of the Hospitaller Order in Malta, the two-year occupation by the French, and the beginning of the British era on the Island.

Like the real and true scholar that he was, Commendatore Fra Antonio Micallef avoided ostentation, and was more prone to charity.

Valletta / Karlsruhe, 2012

Michael Galea   *Wolf-Dieter Barz*

---

[20] Parochial Archives Our Lady of Porto Salvo, Valletta, Libr. Mort. 1805-1830, f. 86v.

Selective Bibliography

Abela, A(lbert) E., "The National Library of Malta", in: *A Nation's Praise - Malta: People, Places and Events*, Malta 1994, 63-82.

Attard, Joseph, *Malta, History of two Millennia*, Valletta (Malta) 2002.

Barbaro di San Giorgio, Mario, *Storia della costituzione del Sovrano Militare Ordine di Malta*, Roma 1927.

Barber, Malcolm (ed.), *The Military Orders* (Vol. I), *Fighting for the Faith and Caring for the Sick*, Aldershot et alt. 1994. – **Nicholson, Helen** (ed.), *The Military Orders* (Vol. II), *Welfare and Warfare*, Aldershot et alt. 1998.

Barz, Wolf-Dieter, "Ein „melitensischer Vatikan" auf Malta?", in: *Der Johanniterorden in Baden-Württemberg*, No. 99, 1999, 23-27.

Burgtorf, Jochen, "Die Herrschaft der Johanniter im Heiligen Land", in: **Czaja, Roman** (ed.), *Die Ritterorden als Träger der Herrschaft, Territorien, Grundbesitz und Kirche*, Torun 2007, 27-57.

Cassar, Paul, *The Holy Infirmary of the Knights of St. John - La Sacra Infermeria*, 3rd ed., Valletta (Malta) 2005.

Cavaliero, Roderick, *The Last of the Crusaders, the Knights of St. John and Malta in the Eighteenth Century*, London 1960.

Clark, Robert M., *The Evangelical Knights of St. John - A History of the Bailiwick of Brandenburg of the Knightly Order of St. John of the Hospital at Jerusalem, known as the Johanniter Order*, Dallas 2003.

Critien, Attilio, *Holy Infirmary Sketches*, Malta 1946.

Ellul Micallef, Roger and **Fiorini, Stanley** (eds.), *Collegium Melitense Quatercentenary Celebrations (1592-1992) - Collected Papers*, (University of Malta), Msida 1992.

Floto, Henning, *Der Rechtsstatus des Johanniterordens - eine rechtsgeschichtliche und rechtsdogmatische Untersuchung zum Rechtsstatus der Balley Brandenburg des ritterlichen Ordens St. Johannis vom Spital zu Jerusalem*, Berlin 2003.

Galea, Michael, *Grandmaster Hughes Loubenx de Verdalle 1582-1595*, San Gwann (Malta) 2000.

Grima, Joseph F., *Printing and Censorship in Malta 1642-1839 - A General Survey*, Valletta (Malta) 1991.

Hellwald, Ferdinand de, *Bibliographie méthodique de L'Ordre Souv(erain) de St. Jean de Jérusalem*, Rome 1885.

Himmels, Heinz, "Der Souveräne Malteser-Ritterorden als Völkerrechtssubjekt", in: *Vertrauen in den Rechtsstaat, Beiträge zur deutschen Einheit im Recht, Festschrift für Walter Remmers*, Köln 1995, 213-230.

Knopf-Silvestre, Frédérique, *L'Ordre Souverain de Malte en Droit International Public*, Toulouse 2000.

Luttrell, Anthony T., *The Hospitaller State on Rhodes and its Western Provinces, 1306-1462*, Aldershot et alt. 1999. - *The Hospitallers of Rhodes and their Mediterranean World*, London 1992.

Mallia-Milanes, Victor (ed.), *Hospitaller Malta 1530-1798 - Studies on Early Modern Malta and the Order of St. John of Jerusalem*, Msida (Malta) 1993.

McHugh, Rosita, The Knights of Malta - 900 Years of Care, Dublin 1996.

Papanti Pelletier de Berminy, Paolo and **Barz, Wolf-Dieter**, "Das neue Verfassungssystem des Souveränen Malteserordens", in: *Jahrbuch des öffentlichen Rechts der Gegenwart*, neue Folge, Vol. 48, 2000, 325-350.

Prantner, Robert, *Malteserorden und Völkergemeinschaft*, Berlin 1974.

Raap, Christian, "Die Kontinuität des Johanniterordens", in: *Iustitia et Pax – Gedächtnisschrift für Dieter Blumenwitz*, Berlin 2008, 1129-1144.

Riley-Smith, Jonathan (ed.), *The Oxford Illustrated History of the Crusades*, Oxford 1995.

Riley-Smith, Jonathan, *Hospitallers - The History of the Order of St. John*, London et alt. 1999.

Sainty, Guy S., *The Orders of St. John - The History, Structure, Membership and modern Role of the five Hospitaller Orders of Saint John of Jerusalem*, New York 1991.

Savona-Ventura, Charles, *Knight Hospitaller Medicine, in Malta, 1530-1798*, San Gwann (Malta) 2004.

Schermerhorn, Elisabeth, *Malta of the Knights*, (new print) London 1978.

Seward, Desmond, *The Monks of War*, London 1972.

Sire, H(enry) J. A., *The Knights of Malta*, New Haven et alt. 1994 (1996).

Sovereign Military and Hospitaller Order of St. John of Jerusalem, Rhodes and Malta, 9th centenary celebrations (L-Ospedalier, the Official Journal of the Maltese Association, December 1999).

Steeb, Christian (ed.), *Der Souveräne Malteser-Ritter-Orden in Österreich*, Graz 1999.

Testa, Carmel, *The Life and Times of Grand Master Pinto 1741-1773*, Valletta (Malta) 1989.

Vella, Andrew P., *The University of Malta - A Bicentenary Memorial*, Malta 1969.

Waldstein-Wartenberg, Berthold, *Rechtsgeschichte des Malteserordens*, Wien et alt. 1969.

Wienand, Adam (ed.), *Der Johanniterorden, der Malteserorden, der ritterliche Orden des hl. Johannes vom Spital zu Jerusalem, seine Geschichte, seine Aufgaben*, 3rd ed., Köln 1988.

Zammit, Themistocles, *L'Universita' di Malta - Origine e Sviluppo*, Malta 1913.

Zammit, William, *Printing in Malta 1642-1839 – Its cultural role from inception to the granting of Freedom of the Press*, Valletta (Malta) 2008.

PART II

LEZIONI

SU

GLI STATUTI

DEL

SAGR'ORDINE GEROSOLIMITANO

NELL' UNIVERSITÁ DEGLI STUDJ

DI

MALTA

PER L'ANNO

1792.

Nella Stamp. del Palazzo di S. A. E. presso Fr. G. M.

MDCCXCII.

Con Licenza de'Superiori

LECTURES ON THE STATUTES OF THE SACRED ORDER OF ST. JOHN OF JERUSALEM

at the University (of Studies) of Malta
1792

At the Printing Press of Fr(a) G(iovanni) M(allia) of the
Palace of H(is) M(ost) E(minent) H(ighness)

MDCCXCII

By Permission of the Superiors

Index

Book One

Book Three

On the third day of October 1791 was read the following petition submitted by the Conventual Chaplain Fr Antonio Micallef, viz

Most Eminent Highness and Sacred Council.

Commendatore Fr Antonio Micallef, Professor of Civil Law in the University of Studies, most humble servant and most obedient religious of Your Most Eminent Highness, with due respect requests that you deign together with this Your Sacred Council remit to the press some of his lectures anent the Statutes of this Sacred Order so as to avoid that he takes the tedious burden of dictating, and to the students that of writing same, and thereby he will be perpetually grateful etc.

His Most Eminent Highness, and the Sacred Council with unanimous consent have entrusted to Commendatore Fr Antonio Miari and Chaplain Com. Fr Maturino Francesco de Müller the task of examining the work of Com. Micallef and of referring back their assessment of this work to the Sacred Council.

On the 9 October 1791 His Most Eminent Highness has substituted Com. Fr Antonio Miari by Com. Fr Michele Benedetto Grimaldi for the purpose of examining the work of Com. Fr Antonio Micallef in terms of the Decree of the Sacred Council of the third of the current month of October.

Ex Lib. Concilior.
Bajul. Fr Lud. D' Almeyda da Portugal Vice-Chancellor.

The 23 of the month of January 1791 *ab Incarnatione*. The Commissioners, deputized to examine the lectures anent the Statutes of this Sacred Council at the University of Malta, and to ascertain whether authorization could be given to the author enabling him to print them, have submitted the following report, namely.

Most Eminent Highness and Sacred Council

We have read the manuscript entitled *Lezioni su gli Statuti di questo Sagr'Ordine nell'Universita' di Malta, per l'anno 1792* (Lectures on the Statutes of the Sacred Order given at the University of Malta during the year 1792) and have the honour to inform Your Most Eminent Highness and this Sacred Council, that these lectures lend much light and much lucidity to the disposition and literal expression of the Statute, and show that the author is deeply versed in our jurisprudence. We also believe that the said work, when it is completed, should by itself eliminate many of those cases which usually occur amongst the Religious of the Order of Jerusalem. Hence we are of the opinion that the printing thereof should be of advantage to the public, and most useful to those of all ranks, who have already been received, or who intend to be received by this Sacred Order. Such is our opinion, which we submit to the most enlightened discernment of Your Most Eminent Highness, and Sacred Council, whilst with the deepest respect we declare ourselves to be the most humble, devout and obedient servants and most obedient Religious .

Com. Fr Michele Benedetto Grimaldi - Com. Fr Maturino Francesco de Müller.

His Most Eminent Highness and the Sacred Council having heard the advice of the Commissioners with unanimous vote have granted to the author the licence enabling him to print the abovementioned lectures, provided that they should not, nor can they ever, be taken as interpreting or explaining the Statutes and Ordinances of Our Sacred Order in any tribunal.

Ex Libr Concilior.

Com. Fr Franciscus de Carvalho Pinto Vicecancellarius Coadjutor.

Book One

Chapter I

Nature of the Sacred Order of Jerusalem

That the Sacred Order of Jerusalem today known as of Malta is a true Religion, is contested clearly in Canon Law (Dritto Canonico) chapter *Cum plantare de Privilegiis*, be that as it may, like all the other claustrals it was disputed by moralists of the past century. A good number shew it (to use their own terms) *secundum quid, et lato modo* appearing strange to them, that a society may consider itself religious, when one of its purposes is militancy, a profession strongly contrary to contemplative life, and away from the noises and dangers of the world; others, convinced by the fact that in the said Sacred Order one makes the solemn profession of the three vows of Chastity, Poverty and Obedience, define the Order as a true and effective Religion. Pope Benedict X1V of immortal memory decided the whole issue with an admirable statement[1] in his Apostolic Letter of the 13 October 1745 to Cardinal Portocarrero couched as follows: *Since you are a knight of Malta professed and true Religious, it did not appear to us logically to have any doubt on the subject; having made in the profession the three solemn vows of Chastity, Poverty and Obedience, and this being the true and common opinion of the authors and of the tribunals, even that of Rome, as can be gleaned from the treatise :* in propugnacolo Ierosolymitano disquis.1.cap.2. *to no avail is the doubt proposed by some that one cannot be a true Religious, who is bound to militancy, and in this respect the teaching of St. Thomas is clear 2.2.qu.288.art.3 which does not repugn the state of true Religion by fighting in defence of divine cult, of the common good, and of the poor and the oppressed, which is precisely the purpose of the Order of Malta, as you very well know.*

---

[1] *Bull. Benedicti XIV. in Supplem. n. 2 tom. 3*

Chapter II

Purposes of the Sacred Order of Jerusalem

The purposes of the Sacred Order are twofold: hospitality and militancy. According to constant tradition which goes back to six centuries, hospitality was established for the first time by the Rector Gerardo; the other was solemnly adopted in 1118 by the Chapter General convened in Jerusalem by the First Master Fr Raimondo de Puy. Padre Paoli in an elegant and erudite dissertation printed in Rome in 1781 maintains that from its inception the Order adopted both purposes; in such instances, everyone is at liberty to make his own judgement.

The Sacred Order practises hospitality by running a vast hospital in its convent in Malta where the sick of all nationality are given shelter. Militancy consists in maintaining ships, galleys and troops in continuous action against the Turk, and particularly to protect trade to all the nations in the Mediterrenean from the piracy of the Barbary States.

Chapter III

The Sovereignty of the Sacred Order

Our Sacred Order carries with it two aspects: the one as a true Religion, and therefore immediately subject to the Holy See; the other as having the character of a Temporal Sovereign in the countries of its residence. It is wrongly believed that the Sacred Order started being a Sovereign Order in 1309, at the time of the conquest of Rhodes, when in fact it became as such from the very moment that it adopted the establishment of militancy. Here is the evidence with the premise the following principles: every civil society which of its own nature and with its laws governs itself without any dependence on others is a Sovereign State; every civil society which by all the Sovereigns is acknowledged as having the right to make war with its owns troops, and to acquire irrevocably the property and states of the enemy, and to contract alliances for attack and defence with other Sovereigns, is a Sovereign State; having a flag respected at sea by the Powers is an univocal proof of the Sovereignty of the government, to which it pertains. With the guidance of these principles there is nothing left but to go through our annals in order to decide on the matter.

The Sacred Order was set up in 1118; we have proven evidence in our history, that since then it governed on its own without the least dependence on the King of Jerusalem, in whose territory it resided. Assembled in Chapter General it promulgated its fundamental laws; this equally means that since then it exercised judicial power, not only on all the individuals who formed part of it, but likewise on all the laymen attached to its military and economic service, by having set up for them a Tribunal, known as Castellania, endowed with mere and mixed jurisdiction.

According to our history in 1134 the Sacred Order maintained at its own expense and command troops, with which Grandmaster Du Puy offered defence to King Baldwin of Jerusalem against the armies of the Caliph of Egypt and King Roldequin of Damascus, auxiliary sovereign.

A short time afterwards and precisely in 1135 the same Grandmaster Du Puy with the forces of his Order conquered Bersabea, recognized at the time as legitimate by King Falque of Jerusalem, appointing subsequently as Governor of the Fortress in the acquired state the Grand Hospitaller Roberto of Maraclen.

According to the document kept in the Vatican archives, in 1206, after the Sacred Order had undertaken the protection of King Licon of Armenia, and stipulated with him a league for attack and defence, it conquered with its troops the city of Salit together with Castelnuovo and Comardo.

If there had not been other proof, the conquest of Rhodes overtly shows the Order as being already sovereign: Grandmaster Folco de Villaret with a squadron of twenty-five galleys flying the banner of the Sacred Order left Brinidisi in Spring 1309 and before the season was over he conquered the island. No expeditions were allowed to one who is no Sovereign.

From 1130, at a time in which Pope Innocent II gave the Sacred Order the banner of the white cross on a red field, up to the conquest of Rhodes all ships of the Sacred Order navigated with that flag recognized by all Sovereigns.

But a king without a kingdom and a sovereign without territory: will there be someone who will not believe it possible: Grozio[2] gives two qualities of objects to sovereignty, primary and secondary: the primary are the people united in the civil society subject to mere and mixed authority, of whom they chose to govern them; the secondary is the territory, wherein the people reside. Moses (says the famous author) was the true and effective monarch of the Jewish People, when he went wandering on the banks of the river Sala.

Chapter IV

Government of the Sacred Order

The punctual observance of the two purposes of the Hospital and of Militancy put in continuous danger its very existence: the solemn vow of obedience requires a blind execution of the commands of the government; the vow of poverty constitutes the Superior as full master of all possessions and acquisitions of every individual. In such a society there can be no other government except one, in which every member has the assured confidence of being preserved from whatsoever abuse of his life

---

[2] *De Jur. Bel. & Pac.*

and property. None of the three types of governments was chosen: obviously not the monarchical because it was subject to frequent changes; the aristocratic because in a short time in a state of the few it can be restricted; the democratic because almost with all nations with the greatest facility it is converted into licence.

Our wise legislators chose a government, which partakes of all three, judging it to be the most secured and the most stable, because (as a famous politician remarks) *the one guards the other being in the same city, the principality, the nobles and the people* - the system of Licurgo, to whom is due the long duration of eight hundred years of the Republic of Sparta, according to the unanimous opinion of the sage.

To realize so well a concieved machinery the government was at first divided into four nations: French, Italian, Spanish and English; from these were formed the first seven Bodies known as Langues: they are Provence, Auvergne, France, Italy, Spain, England and Alemagne.

In 1462 from that of Spain was dismembered an eighth one with the name of Castile and Portugal, and therefore the Spanish was henceforth called of Aragon.

To each of these eight Langues was assigned a chief, known as Pilier or Conventual Bailiff with particular titles: that of the Langue of Provence, Grand Commendator; that of Auvergne, Marshal; of France, Hospitaller; of Italy, Admiral; of Aragon, Grand Conservator; of England, Turcopolier; of Alemagne, Grand Bailiff; of Castile, Grand Chancellor, all being elevated in dignity.

As the interests of the Sacred Order required many Knights and Religious to reside in the Provinces, where the Order had its estates, in each was established a body by the name of Provincial Chapter having at its head a Prior.

Finally our founders thought it also expedient that in the Provinces there should be Religious elevated in dignity, and there were established, besides the Priors, others with the title of Capitular Bailiffs.

The total number of these dignities rising up to fifty-two was divided equally among the four nations, allotting 13 to each.

On this basis was established the legislative power with the principles of democracy, judicial power with those of aristocracy, and the executive with those of monarchy. Thus in this manner are our Tribunals organized.

Chapter V

The Sacred Chapter General

The supreme legislator of the Sacred Order is the Chapter General as laid down by the first Statute of this title. It is made up of the Grandmaster, the Bishop, the Prior of the Conventual Church representing the clergy, the Conventual Bailiffs, the Priors, the Capitular Bailiffs, the Bailiffs *ad honores*, a Procurator for each Langue, a Procurator for each Provincial Chapter. It is an assembly of the whole Sacred Order. Individuals and subaltern bodies have their own representatives.

All the abovementioned embodied in the Chapter General have to be present under the strict penalty of deprivation of the habit *Stat. III. del Capitolo*, moderated by the Grandmaster and the Sacred Council *Stat. IV.*, excepted in case they are unable to attend for a legitimate reason, and are therefore obliged to appoint a Procurator *Stat. III. above*.

This Tribunal so numerous was not considered proper to create and establish laws. It was stipulated by *Stat. I. del Capitolo* that the members forming this assembly divided in Langues should choose by secret vote two members for each Langue, that is, Sixteen. Those elected take the oath in the hand of the Grandmaster and of the Chapter to establish -

having put apart all personal regard - all that, which they will judge useful and honourable to the Sacred Order, and to the Brethren. And hence Grandmaster and Chapter draw up all deliberations as will be taken by the Sixteen.

The Sixteen, called the Chapter members (*capitolanti*), retire in a place destined for the Chapter; with them intervene the Procurator of the Grandmaster having an advisory vote, the Vice-Chancellor to register the deliberations *Stat. I. del Capitolo*, and the Secretary to the Treasury *Ordinaz. 23 dello stesso Tit.*

Their first act is to take solemn oath for maintaining the highest secrecy of all that which is proposed and concluded when in session. The Procurator of the Grandmaster takes the oath with reservation, enabling him to communicate all the proceedings to the Grandmaster.

The authority of the Sixteen is limited only to legislation; it is forbidden to them to discuss particular interests; with the reservation that the Chapter takes cognizance of such interests; it is similarly prohibited to grant favours. Caravita in his compendium title 16 para. 3 says, that, according to ancient custom, *they can concede favours to the Grandmaster, who requests them through his Procurator.*

Each Body and any participant in the Chapter may freely formulate projects which in our language are called roles (*ruoli*), on every branch of government, supported by the signature of the proposer, and they are all referred to the Sixteen for their examination.

The Complete Council, after notice of the holding of the Chapter has been served, refers to eight Commissioners, one for each Langue, so that together with the Procurators of the Treasury, Treasurer General, Conventual Conservator, Procurator of the Grandmaster, Vice-Chancellor, and Secretary to the Treasury, they may draw up the public role, that is, they examine the entire existing legislation, the manner of administering public business, and may provide the means of eliminating prejudices, and of remedying the defects existing therein.

Our Code does not lay down the time for holding a Chapter General; the circumstances of the times determine that, although in each convocation is fixed the day for holding the subsequent Chapter. In the Chapter General of 1631 it was indicated to celebrate the next one in 1641, but in fact it was held in 1776. Only in case of a threatening siege or other urgent necessity of the Sacred Order such as a new extraordinary imposition should be made on the commanderies, as prescribed by *Ordin. 6. del Tesoro*, which contemporaneaously announces the celebration of the Chapter for the ensuing year; if for some cause the Chapter cannot be convened, such convocation is held a year after the impediment is removed.

To participate in the Chapter General one has to be a professed knight, has resided five years in the Convent, being the period equivalent for those employed in the service of the Sacred Order as Receiver and Procurator of the Treasury, and not being in debts with the said Treasury *Stat. IX. Ordinaz. 6 del Capit. Stat XLIX. del Tesoro.*

In the week preceding the opening of the Chapter the Ordinary Sacred Council deputizes four Commissioners of different nationality entrusted to examine and acknowledge all documents *Ord. 8. del Capitolo*, that is, to ascertain whether they are submitted in authentic form *Stat. V. del Capitolo*, and in accordance with the forms indicated in the *Statuti VI. e VII. del medesimo titolo.*

It is prohibited in *Stat. IX* to appoint a Procurator with power to substitute.

Participants in the Chapter who are absent and are authorized to appoint attorneys must appoint Religious of their rank, in such a manner that the knight cannot have as his attorney a Chaplain or a Servant-at-Arms *Ordin. 5. del Capitolo.*

The Chapter General lasts fifteen effective days with power to the Sixteen to extend this term for another eight days, should circumstances so require *Stat. XVI. and XVII. del Capitolo.*

The Chapter winds up with the publication by the Vice Chancellor of the new legislation compiled by the Sixteen, together with the functions described in *Stat. I. di questo titolo.*

Chapter VI

Continuation

From the context of all the Statutes included in the title of Chapter General, one notes, that this Tribunal has the power to grant favours, and especially from *Stat.XV. del Capitolo*, where favours subreptitiously and abreptitiously obtained are declared null and void, and from *Ordin.25 dello stesso titolo*, in which two thirds of the votes are required in order to consider the favour as granted.

Similarly it is recognized that either Body or Individual has the liberty of making recourse for his private interests, whilst in terms of *Stat. I., ed Ord. 10 del Capitolo* the commission of four members is entrusted to examine such submissions.

Considering that these are many or that proferring a sentence entails necessarily a long examination, the Chapter General can and usually does remit the decision to the Sacred Complete Council, known as the Reserve Council *(Consiglio delle Ritenzioni)*. Moreover from *Stat. XVI.* under the same title it appears that if a matter submitted to the Chapter has not been decided, the Complete Council has, indeed, the power to decide such matter, even if it has not been submitted to it by the Chapter General.

Chapter VII

Judicial Power

1. Within the Sacred Order two Tribunals are vested with judicial power: that which in legal jargon is termed at first instance, known as Ordinary Council; that of appeals, known as Complete Council.

2. The Ordinary Council is strictly made up of the Grandmaster and the eight Piliers: that is, the Grand Commendator, the Marshal, the Grand Hospitaller, the Admiral, the Grand Conservator, the Turcopolier, the Grand Bailiff, the Grand Chancellor.

3. Without these the Council cannot be convened; and in case of an impediment of any one of them or of not wanting to participate therein, the same Council must appoint an attorney before starting its proceedings, *Stat.I. di questo titolo.*

4. An ancient custom converted into Statute, which is the *First of the Council,* fixed the members for this Senate: the Prior of the Conventual Church, all the Priors, the Capitular Bailiffs. The transfer of these islands to the Sacred Order by Emperor Charles V included also the Bishop.

5. Of all these, except for the Bishop and the Prior of the Church, one could freely say that they have the right to participate in the Council but in fact they are never present or at least few of them, since our laws prescribe the residence of the Priors in the limits of their dignity as local superiors outside the Convent, and of the Capitular Bailiffs in the bailliwicks entrusted to them. The *Stat. II. del Consiglio* requires only three Priors to reside in the Convent, each for two years, in turn as enjoined by the Grandmaster.

6. Consequently according to this system the Council would consist of the Grandmaster as President, of the Conventual Bailiffs or Piliers, of the Bishop, of the Prior of the Conventual Church, and of three Priors, these

being the minor portion of the Brotherhood; hence this assembly is an aristocratic Senate. If it is true, as most true is the principle, that when power whether sovereign or judicial is in the hands of a certain number of citizens it is called aristocracy: this is the proof of the second conclusion brought forth in *Capitolo* 4.

7. Since some centuries Bailiffs have been introduced known as *ad honores*, who are promoted to this dignity by Papal Brief.

8. Also equally included in this Tribunal are the Vice Chancellor, the Seneschal, and the Captain General of the Galleys; and as the first two are not Bailiffs, they have an advisory vote. The General, however, being a Knight Little Cross, has a deciding vote only in matters relating to the government of the Sacred Order, and not in other particular matters both civil and criminal - *Stat.I.del Consiglio, and Ordin.7. delle Galere.*

The same Senate has the power to choose in a definite manner the members forming it *Stat. III. dell'Elezione*, limited however to whom is provided with a public document as to his merits issued by his Langue, and to the requisites regarding residence in the Convent, and the Commanderies and other matters as will be indicated later.

None of the Councillors can be admitted in the Council, unless he has first taken the oath in terms of the form expressed in *Ordin. 6. del Consiglio.*

Such oath is considered tacitly taken by him who is called to substitute in the Council the Piliers who are absent *Ordin. 7 dello stesso titolo.*

The Sacred Ordinary Council is absolutely the Tribunal of first instance in litigations regarding Precedence, Pre-eminence, Elections to Conventual Dignitites, Promotions to Priorates and Bailliwicks, reception of Commanderies and validity of pensions; consequently the hearing of the litigation starts there.

However, the same Sacred Council adjudicates appeals from sentences proffered by the Provincial Chapters, and from those by Commissioners, deputized by the Grandmaster, who, as will be subsequently explained, has the pre-eminence of deputizing in the first instance Commissioners in private civil disagreements anent credits, *et similia*, as well as from sentences proffered by the Chamber of Accounts (*Camera dei Conti*), and from Deliberations taken by the Langues *Stat. XXXVI. del Consiglio.*

The plurality of votes constitutes in this Tribunal the sentence or provision *Stat. XIII. del Consiglio;* in case of parity, which we call equilibrium, if the Council is judging at first instance, the matter is referred to the Complete Council; if it is judging in appeal, then the sentence is confirmed from which the appeal was interposed *Stat. XIV. del Consiglio.*

If the equilibrium occurs in the Secret Council, the matter is treated afresh; the Council has so determined on two occasions namely on 11. and 26. January 1665 ab.Inc.; if in the Criminal Council the sentence proffered is considered to conform to the most favourable advice to the crime *Ordin. 24 del Consiglio.*

Should parity occur in elections for the filling of offices or dignities we have in *Stat. XIV. del Consiglio* the following disposition: *preference is given to the senior person and not to the Fiernaldo* [junior] *if both are Knights Little Cross; but if the Fiernaldo is a Bailiff he should be preferred.* By Bailiff here it is intended (in my opinion) Capitular Bailiffs and not those *ad honores* since at the time of Grandmaster Homedes, when the Statute above cited was promulgated Bailiffs *ad honores* did not exist. If the candidates are of the same seniority the election is referred to the Sacred Complete Council.

Besides judicial power in civil matters, this Sacred Council is also invested with authority to punish crimes, and to decide on all matters, both economical and political, of the State; moreover by Decrees of the same Council dated 28. February 1583 and 15. October 1779 it is gleaned that it has power to promulgate Capitular Ordinances. When it is convened to judge crimes, it is called *Ordinary Criminal Council*; when it is convened to deal with other indicated matters it is called Ordinary Secret Council.

Stat. XIV. del Consiglio requires all sentences are proffered by secret ballot and that it prescribes all kind of provision; moreover *Ord. 22 dello stesso titolo* requires that all the councillors cast their vote in such a manner that at such voting one should ensure that the number of ballots tallies with the number of Councillors present; in case of discrepancy the voting has to be repeated. For this purpose the ballots are of three colours: white, black for the decision, and red for the undecided.

Chapter VIII

Complete Council

The Tribunal of appeals in contentious matters arising from sentences proffered by the Ordinary Council is called Complete Council - *Stat. XXIX. del Cons.*

Forming this Tribunal, apart from all the individuals of the Ordinary Council, sixteen other Knights Little Cross, two for each Langue but in the two Langues of Alemagne and of Castile there are the particular *Ordinaz. 5 and 49 del Consiglio* which for the former, one has to be of the Priorate of Alemagne and the other of the Priorate of Böhmen; for the latter, one has to be Castillian and the other Portuguese; according to *Ordinaz.5 del Consiglio* they have to be professed knights, have reached the age of at least twenty-five years, and have resided in the Convent for five years.

The Alemanni, Bohemian, Castillian and Portuguese in terms of the quoted *Ordinaz .5* have the privilege of being admitted without the requisite of the 5-year residence: this (the text says) because they may not alter the unanimity between Castillians and Portuguese, and between the Alemanni and Bohemians.

Each Langue has the right to appoint and choose its two senior members; the terms of *Ordinaz. 5 del Consiglio* appeared indicative, that the Langues had the free choice of these their representatives in the Sacred Complete Council, in such manner that they could prefer in concourse of many the Fiernaldo [junior] to the senior; but the Sagra Ruota Romana in several deliberations in litigations *Melvitana Consiliaratus such as that of 7. April 1788, 30. March 1789, 11. December 1789* did not adjudicate free this selection, having decided that the senior amongst the candidates who has all the requisites of the cited Ordinance should always be given preference.

This supreme Tribunal is privately vested with the power to elect the Captain in charge of the troops and of the army, the Castellan, the Conventual Conservator, the Procurators of the indigent; likewise the same Tribunal determines to make peace or truce, whether artillery should be recruited from the islands belonging to the Sacred Religion, and to grant permission to Priors and Bailiffs to leave the Convent in order to go abroad, and to confirm favours granted by the Langues, and by the Priorates.

Here, as in the Ordinary Council, applies the general rule, that the plurality of votes establishes the sentence, or other provision, but at the election of the Captain of the troops and of the army as well as in confirming the favours granted by the Langues, in terms of *Stat.12. dell'Elez.* and of *Ordinaz.4. del Ricev.o* and *Ordinaz.39 del Cons.o* three fourths of the votes are necessary.

In case of parity of votes regarding the sentences pronounced by the Ordinary Council these are considered as confirmed; if there occurs equilibrium anent the article, whether appeal from the sentence of the Sacred Ordinary Council should be admitted, in that case *Ordinaz 23 del Consiglio* prescribes a rehearing by the same Tribunal.

We do not have special sanction in case there is in the Complete Council parity of votes in lawsuits devolving to it because of equilibrium in the Ordinary Council; but it appears natural that it should be re-heard by the same Complete Council; whereas should it be proceeded with according to the system, that with equilibrium the litigation is considered devolved to the Tribunal superior to that, which left it undecided, this should be the Chapter General, which in one and a half centuries was convened twice; as a result of little avail would be Our Legislators' solicitude to decide with the least delay disputes among Brethren - *Stat.I. dello Sguardio.*

We have a Complete Council by the name of [Council of] State, made up of the same individuals; they assemble after the demise of Grandmasters to deal with and conclude all matters relating to the Magisterium, with the particular circumstance, that its decisions count as if they have been promulgated by the Chapter General - *Stat. I. dell'Elez.* It is prohibited by *Stat. II. del Maestro* from interlocuting either to derogate or to restrict the Preemenences, Privileges, Prerogatives, and Rights of the Grandmaster: legislation established since 1639 and established by Papal Brief of 2. May 1646 at the instance of Grandmaster Lascaris.

Criminal Council and *Sguardio* [Court of summary jurisdiction] will be dealt with under the titles Crimes and Penalties.

Chapter IX

Inferior Tribunals

Our Sacred Order has diverse types of inferior Tribunals to the two Sacred Councils: in the Convent there are the Langues, the Chamber of Accounts of the Common Treasury, of the Debtors, of the Spoils, and of Legitimacy and Nobility; outside the Convent there are the Chapters and the Provincial Assemblies.

Chapter X

Langues

The Langues of the Sacred Order are called Nations according to *Stat. VIII delle Signif. delle Parole*, but as stated by Caravita[3] the name Langues generally means in all the other Statutes the Congregations which make up the same Nations; strictly speaking the Langues are not Tribunals, whilst as such are meant those vested with the jurisdiction to adjudicate disputes arising between plaintiff and accused, qualities which those do not have as their incumbency is limited to deliberate on Receptions, Assignments of Commanderies and manner of administering the estates of the Sacred Order situated in their respective countries, and to give their opinion, whenever so requested.

Each Langue consists of the Pilier, and of all the Brother Knights, Conventual Chaplains, and Servants-at-Arms.

The requisites to be therein admitted to cast a vote are those of having professed and of having resided for three years in the Convent[4], excepted are those of the Langue of Alemagne and Anglo-Bavarian which completely replaced the extinct Langue of England.

Without the permission of the Grandmaster the Langues cannot be convened, and without notification in advance to all the individuals of the day and time of assembling, indicating to all in writing the matters on which it is deemed expedient to deliberate; all this under pain of rendering null and void the deliberations.

To the Pilier pertains the exclusive right of asking the Grandmaster for permission to convene the respective Langue.

---

[3] *Nel Compend. tit. 7 cap. II*
[4] *Stat. XXXVII. Del Cons.*

Consequent to these principles it is incumbent on all the eight Langues to comply with the following method:

Before convening the Langue the Pilier is bound to communicate to one of the Procurators the matters, for which he thinks proper to hold the assembly.

Then the Secretary informs of the day and time of the meeting, and each item proposed for discussion; such notice duly signed by the Procurators, and Secretary is submitted to the Grandmaster, either by the Pilier himself, or by one of the Procurators asking for permission to convene the Langue[5].

This notification is brought by the Donat of the Langue to the notice of all the Knights, and other professed and authorized Religious.

At the appointed time the meeting is declared open; and in case there is not sufficient number, it is encumbent on the Pilier, or the senior President to call Knights or Religious of another Langue[6]; what may constitute this sufficient number to hold the meeting is not prescribed by Law; each Langue has its own particular usage; in the case of the Langue of Italy there should be at least seven including the Chief.

The items for discussion are proposed by the Pilier[7] but ordinarily the proposals are read article by article as indicated in the notification, deliberating on each item.

All the deliberations are made by secret ballot[8] but since in the Law which lays down this formality there is no provocative decree, it often happens that when there is unanimity, no balloting is resorted to, except for the Langue of Alemagne, where there is the most exact observance of balloting also in regard to the most minute matters.

---

[5] *Cons. 24. October 1639*
[6] *Stat. XXXVIII. del Cons.*
[7] *Stat. XXXVI. del Cons.*
[8] *Ordinaz. 40. Cons.*

All the deliberations are put down in writing and recorded in a Register. Who challenges the truthfulness of the acts therein recorded would be liable to punishment[9]. The Secretary sees to the publication of the contents of all the deliberations.

This publication is considered by the Sagra Ruota Romana[10] as follows:

"Publicatio hujusmodi non pertinet ad essentiam deliberationis, sed est fides & probatio actus jam gesti, & sequi solet in fine Linguae, & postquam expedita sunt omnia negotia in illo congressu resoluta, & pertinet ad solemnitatem". In such manner that for each article proposed in the same session an irrevocable deliberation is taken by ballot.

Immediately the Pilier, or President together with two Procurators must refer to the Grandmaster the contents of all that has been deliberated upon. The decree of the Sacred Council of the 12. September 1639 prescribed that with the Pilier and the Procurators not more than two other Brothers may accompany them.

The Langues are empowered to grant favours, limited by the constant observance in the following matters:

1 st To those pretending to be received in the Sacred Order in each of the three grades to avail themselves of the proofs of relatives, under the condition to justify the consanguinity and identity of the families either in the Convent or outside also without checking the documents with the originals.

2 nd To compile the process of the Visitation of Improvements by only one Commissioner.

3 rd To receive in the dignity of Knights of Justice with postponement of giving proofs of nobility and legitimacy, which favour is always considered granted without prejudice to the seniority of those, who are received with the necessary requisites during the postponement.

---

[9] *Stat. VII. Cons.*

[10] *Melev. Marescallat. 24. Apr. 1716 avant, Cerro.*

4 th To enable those, who are not so entitled for not having resided in the Convent, to cast their vote in the Chapters General and Provincial Assemblies; and in the recent years there were rare instances whereby concession of ballotting was granted for this type of incapacity.

5 th Whenever in any Priorate it would be impossible to convene both the Chapter and the Provincial Assembly, in such case the commission could be sent from the Convent for the purpose of compiling the Proofs[11].

In order that such concessions may be considered granted, it is expedient to obtain two thirds of the votes, and likewise that they are confirmed by the Complete Council with three fourths of the votes[12]. Moreover the concessions abovementioned relating to the Proofs of those being received, in order that they may be valid, it is indispensable that they are confirmed by the first Sacred Complete Council, which is held after the attainment of those concessions.

The Langues like all the Tribunals are included in the general sanction of the *Stat. XLI del Consiglio*, that is to say, that they cannot meet on the feast days therein indicated; however, excepted are the cases en-visaged in the decree of the Sacred Council of 23. August 1656, couched in the following terms:

"Having to declare, as it is just, what is the business, for which the Venerable Langues and Priorates may assemble on feast days in honour of God, of the Bessed Virgin, and of the other Saints, taking into consideration the irreparable prejudices they may cause to many, for not assembling on such days, and the limitation, which is good, that may be imposed on lax practice which had been introduced since some recent years; the Lieutenant and the Venerable Council having taken cognizance of the Report by the Prior of Hungary Fra Franz von Sonnenberg, Bailiff of Aquila Fra Ottaviano Bandinelli, Bailiff of Lora, Fra D. Tommaso de Hobzes, and Bailiff Fra Baldassare de Demandolx Commissioners appointed for the purpose on 29. April ultimo, and complying to

---

[11] *Ordinaz. 2 ddel Ricev. de'Fratelli*
[12] *Ordinaz. e Ricev. e 39. Cons.*

their advice, by ballot they have decreed that the said Venerable Langues and Priorates may assemble on such days only to deal with matters relating to Dignities, Commanderies, Seniority of justice, Presentation of Proofs, Improvements, and all other writings concerning ability and seniority".

Each Langue has its own Procurators who are two in number and appointed every two years, without regard to seniority; only the Langue of France has three: one for each Priorate, that is of France, Aquitaine and Champagne.

To the Procurators of the Langues is strictly prohibited by *Ordinaz.6 delle Probizioni e Pene* to make any protest, recourse or any other act on behalf of the respective Langue without an expressed order by the Langue, under penalities being inflicted by the Statutes against the disobedient.

In all the eight Langues there is a second type of assembly, which is called *Colletta*: this is held for matters which can be called domestic, that is to say, concern the particular management of the Langue in which the public of the Sacred Order is not interested[13]. According to old established custom it is convoked with permission of the Pilier alone.

The *Collette* are empowered by *Ordinaz. XLVI del Cons.* to contract life annuities of members belonging to the respective Langues for the professed Knights and up to nine years for the novices.

Also in the *Collette* plurality of votes constitutes the deliberation; and the execution of the deliberation may be suspended if there is a complaint; however, if the provision has been taken with two thirds of the votes, it is carried into execution notwithstanding any complaint[14].

---

[13] *Stat. XXXIX del Cons.*
[14] *Ordinaz. 47 del Cons.*

Chapter XI

Chamber of Accounts (*Camera dei Conti*)

The Exchequer of the Sacred Council, that is to say, the public money, in the style of the ancient Romans is called Comun Tesoro (Common Treasury).

In view that in all cultured nations the Exchequer has a judge with the exclusive jurisdiction to decide, at first instance, all its disputes, our Legislators had established a Collegial Tribunal, calling it Chamber of Accounts (*Camera dei Conti*). It is not known exactly when it was set up but Caravita[15] thinks it came into being in 1440; others think differently, but this does not merit further examination.

One of the Fiscal Privileges is that the Exchequer also as plaintiff must be tried by its judge or exclusive Tribunal, against the rules, that the plaintiff must be brought to court for the crime committed. Caravita[16] justifies that the Chamber of Accounts possesses as of old the right to plead to itself all lawsuits relating to the Treasury introduced in other Tribunals, both secular and of the Sacred Order with the following decrees proffered indeed by the same Venerable Chamber, but in face of the Government, which always remains silent; the following are the precise terms of the Author:

"From the Castellania the Ven. Chamber on behalf of the Common Treasury, as successor to the spoils of Bailiff Cagnolo, pleaded the lawsuit, which was being treated at the Castellania between Aloisetta Sorda, regarding a house sold to her by the said Bailiff, and Lorenza Majorchina advancing a claim on the said house - *Aud. Cam. 11. Febr. 1621*".

"The Grandmaster pleaded and remitted to the Ven. Chamber the claim lodged with the Castellania by Dr. Federico Falzon versus Fra Natale Armengual as proprietor of a house, to which the Common Treasury was in part successor, *Aud. Cam. 13 Luglio 1675*".

---

[15] *Del Tesoro Cap. 38. Punt. 1 n. 26*
[16] *Cap. 38 punt. 1 n. 10 e seg.*

"The Ven. Chamber on behalf of the Treasury as heir of the spoils of Admiral Capponi pleaded the lawsuit, which was being heard by the Castellania between said Admiral and the sons of Orlando Abejer. *Aud. 19 April 1670*".

"From the Commissioners as deputies of the Grandmaster the Ven. Chamber on behalf of the Common Treasury, as successor to the spoils of Commandeur Fra Ramiro de las Cueras, pleaded to itself the lawsuit, which was being dealt with between said Commandeur and Gregorio Grimaldi before the Commissioners deputized by the Grandmaster. *Aud. Cam. 4 April 1609*".

"The Ven. Chamber on behalf of the Treasury, as successor to the spoils of the Prior of France Saint Osanges, pleaded to itself the lawsuit pending before the Commissioners as deputies of the Grandmaster between Giovanni Rovest, for a previous lawsuit and delegated the same Commissioners already deputized. *Aud. Cam. 28. Sept. 1641*".

"From the Commissioners for lawsuits, the Ven. Chamber on behalf of the Treasury, as successor to the spoils of Bailiff of the Morea Saccomuille, pleaded to itself the lawsuit pending before the Commissioners for immovables between Barbara Castelletta and Commandeur Fra Ottaviano Buttigella, owner of the house of said Bailiff Saccomuille, whose spoils he was entitled to receive for damages. *Aud. Cam. 22. April 1616 & 10. Febr. 1618*".

"Of other judges outside the Council, the Ven. Council declared null and void a sentence preferred by the Court of the Commandery of Modica between Baroness Donna Antonia de Grimaldis and Lucia de Guarassi as sister and heiress of the Chaplain Fra Vincenzo Giarratana, following the demise of Fra Vincenzo recognition pertained to the Council and to the Treasury successor in his spoils; however the Ven. Chamber pleaded to itself that lawsuit and deputized therefore Commissioners. *Aud Cam. 9. Dicemb. 1634*".

"And Commandeur Averoldo having pretended from the Ven. Council, that a pension constituted by the Prior of Messina Martelli on the commandery of Castellazzo be declared null and void in favour of Commandeur Pazzi, which then devolved on him (Averoldo), and there being deputized Commissioners in Council on 28 November 1605. And as Commandeur Pazzi deceased when the dispute was still pending, the matter was referred to the Ven. Chamber, to which pertained that interest after said demise. The Chamber then proffered sentence on 4 April 1609. All the above appears also more clearly in the registers of the delegated lawsuits, which are kept at the Treasury. *Tom.2 n.3*".

"This privilege of pleading to itself lawsuits always takes place whenever a lawsuit concerns the Exchequer, and it assists as plaintiff, that is, when the accused signifies dispute to the plaintiff, that is to him, from whom he acquired that property for which he is summoned for the purpose of being able to have regress for the eviction *ubi supra n. 703*. And although some deny this privilege to the Exchequer *apud Furgos.de Regim tom. disp.4 n. 353* in any case the Ven.Chamber has always enjoyed this privilege, as appears from the following examples:"

"The Ven. Chamber on behalf of the Treasury as successor of the spoils of the Prior of Messina La Marra pleaded the lawsuit which Giovanna Viva Montana tried against Commandeurs Macedonio and Cordines, as pledges by the said Prior La Marra, whose spoils were hypothecated to make good for damages. *Aud. Cam.12. Febr. 1663*".

"The Grandmaster at the instance of the Procurator of lawsuits pleaded and remitted to the Ven. Chamber the dispute moved by Michele Cadamosto versus Donna Antonia Caloriti, and Bologna owner of a house acquired by him from Bailiff Fra Giorgio Fortunio, who had transmitted to the said Procurator of lawsuits bill claiming the extinction of the spoils of said Bailiff. *Aud. Cam. 9. November 1641*".

"The Grandmaster pleaded and remitted to the Ven. Chamber the dispute which D. Diego Damico moved against Commandeur Fra Ottavio Tancredi regarding a house sold to him by the Treasury. *Aud. Cam. 11. Sept. 1671*".

"The Grandmaster pleaded and remitted to the Ven. Chamber the lawsuit currently being treated by the Commissioners deputized by him between Commandeur Orsi and Gabuccini regarding cattle, which said Conmandeur Gabuccini had bought from the Common Treasury, but had transmitted laudatory bill to the Procurator of lawsuits. *Aud. Cam. ubi supra*".

"The Grandmaster pleaded and remitted to the Ven. Chamber the lawsuit introduced in the Castellania by Giovanni Filippo Micallef regarding a house owned by Flaminia Valente, who satisfied the Treasury, as owner of several magazines burdened prior to the eviction and indemnity of Valente. *Aud. Cam. ubi supra*".

"The Grandmaster pleaded and remitted to the Ven. Chamber the claim introduced in the Castellania by Francesco Xuereb anent a house owned by Giorgio Salemi, who satisfied the Treasury as successor of Grandmaster Redin i.e. from the spoils. *Aud. Cam. ubi supra*".

"Moreover it is the privilege of the Treasury to acknowledge disputes which arise among private persons, when they are lawsuits dependent on the Exchequer. Carleval. *ubi supra no.707*. And conforming thereto the Ven. Chamber has always conducted its proceedings".

"And thus a Commandeur claiming to have paid to the Receiver, who denied him, the Ven. Chamber deputized Commissioners, although the Treasury had liquid credit, and it was only being disputed, who of the two was the true debtor. Whence it was ordained, that in that dispute the Procurator of lawsuits should not intervene, provided in one way or other the Common Treasury should be entirely satisfied of its credit. *Aud. Cam. 27. October 1607*".

"And in a similar controversy between Commandeur Badat and Receiver Roero the Ven. Chamber had equally deputized Commissioners, and many other examples one can read in the registers of the Treasury *Aud. Cam. 15. July 1645, 27. March 1666, 9. August 1670*".

"Moreover a Brother quarrelling in the Council with two others who had already been Receivers anent the administration of some Commanderies, the Ven. Council declared that the congizance of that lawsuit pertained in first instance to the Ven Chamber. *27. May 1699*".

"Finally the Exchequer succeeding to the property after commencement of claim, is not bound to follow the first judge, but can terminate it at his Tribunal".

"One generally limits this conclusion meaning that the succession of the Exchequer may be by title of inheritance, because then it represents the deceased person - *utitur Jure suo* - as per law *Fisc. ff. de Jure Fisci*. It can bring the lawsuit to its court when this happens in virtue of publication or confiscation of property, because then it does not represent the person of the deceased, but of the direct owner, and thus it does not appear as successor but as owner. *Carleval ubi supra n. 316 recent.Decis.396*".

"Secondly, the above conclusion is limited to some, meaning that the Exchequer succeeding to the property may plead the lawsuit, when it succeeds to the plaintiff, but not when it succeeds to the accused, which limitation by Tonduto and others is disputed, proving that indistinctly the Exchequer may plead the lawsuit or may succeed to the plaintiff or to the accused. *Tondut. de Praevent Part.1.cap.30 n.70*".

"Thirdly, finally it is limited by others who want that there be the pleading of the Exchequer, when it succeeds during the first instance, but in the stage of appeal, when sentence is already proffered, which limitation supported by *Saliceto* and others is commonly refused as false by *Carleval. ubi supra n.714*".

"But the Ven. Chamber through the death of its Brethren has always pleaded to itself lawsuits, which in their lifetime were pending before other judges or Tribunals, as appears from the examples abovementioned. Not opposing the first limitation though commonly accepted, because the Religion succeeding to the spoils of its Brethren, does not succeed to the person, but to the property, because all that is acquired after profession is acquired for the Religion; on the contrary the acquisition is made over to the Religion and not to the Religious, as has decided the *Sagra Ruota part.1.recent. decis. 333*. And this is not only according to disposition of the *Stat. X dei Contratti*, but also of the Jus Commune, since in another place the same Sagra Ruota *coram Ludovis. Decis. 87 per tot.* and in *Aut de Monarchis 55. Si quis autem* openly disposes, that against the Religion which has the direct ownership (*dominio*) of the property of the Religious, no action is taken, as against successor but as owner. - *Jure proprio*".

"And the Ven. Chamber has made this pleading of lawsuits through the death of our Brethren, whether the Treasury was the plaintiff or accused as is manifest from the above examples".

"Though the lawsuit was in appeal or about to be so lodged in appeal, as one gleans from the following case. Vincenzo Zarb won against Commandeur Giovanbattista Montalto two sentences from the judges deputized by the Grandmaster; the said Commandeur feeling himself aggrieved by the latter sentence, lodged an appeal, and were deputized other Commissioners, before whom both of them having brought forward their reasons, at the conclusion there occurred the death of the said Commandeur and the said Zarb demanded either to stay by the last sentence or that the Procurator of lawsuits makes up his mind to terminate the said lawsuit. And the Ven. Chamber determined, that it stayed by that which was declared by the Judges delegated by the Grandmaster, freeing the Treasury from whatsoever claim by the said Zarb for debit interests from the said lawsuit. *Aud. Cam. 10. May 1625*".

"As regards the form adopted in similar pleadings up to the month of November 1641 the Ven. Chamber always pleaded every lawsuit pertaining to the Common Treasury *Aud. Cam. 9. November 1641*, but since then it has been introduced that the Procurator of lawsuits submitted a petition to the Grandmaster so that pleading to himself the lawsuit, he would remit it to the Ven.Chamber to adjudicate it; and ever since this has always been the practice, except in the pleading made on the 19 April 1670 mentioned above".

"But in lawsuits introduced in the Magistrato degli Armamenti (Magistrate for Armaments) the Treasury does not have the privilege to plead such lawsuits, as having an interest in the spoils of the Religious; it was so declared by the Sacred Council on *18 November 1633*".

The Camera dei Conti (Chamber of Accounts) is made up of the Grand Commandator, the two Procurators of the Treasury, the Treasurer General, the Procurator of the Grandmaster at the Treasury, and sixteen professed knights - two for each Langue called Uditori dei Conti (Auditors of Accounts); eight however are in the exercise of their employment, the other eight , who are known as substitutes, are meant to supplement the first ones wherever these are hindered from intervening in the Tribunal; the Secretary for the Treasury and the Advocates and Procurators of lawsuits of the Treasury, Religious and Secular, these however have a simple consultative vote.

Ordinaz. 90 del Tesoro prescribes the register for recording therein all the sentences pronounced by the Tribunal. And *Ordinaz. 44 dello stesso Titolo* that requests which have been rejected cannot be further re-proposed.

From the contents of *Stat. XLVIII Tesoro* and the cited *Ordinaz. 44* it appears that they refer to sentences in judicial disputes; whilst it is uniform to the principles of common law, that the same judge cannot re-examine the sentence proffered by him but in all other business, wherein the deliberation is not a sentence, he can without fault re-examine it and annul it.

The Grand Commendatore is the Chief and President of this Tribunal, therefore he precedes everybody, excepted the only instance when at the meeting there intervenes the Lieutenant of the Grandmaster. Amongst the other Bailiffs, each one precedes according to his dignity; consequently if the Procurator of the Grandmaster is preminent, he precedes the Procurators of the Treasury[17]. When the Grand Commendator is absent from the Convent, and is represented by his Lieutenant, he undersigns after the Procurators of the Treasury[18]; the Knight who intervenes in the Chamber of Accounts sent by the Grand Commendator or his Lieutenant, in his stead, precedes and takes his place according to his seniority in the Religion, vis-a-vis the *Uditori dei Conti* (Auditors of Accounts)[19].

Singular are the formalities which *Ordinaz. 84 sotto il Titolo del Comun. Tesoro* prescribes to the Ven. Langues in the choice, that is, appointment of these Uditori. The Langue is to be notified three days in advance of the day fixed by the Pilier for the nomination of the abovementioned Uditori. On each individual of the respective Langues is imposed the obligation to be present under pain of not being allowed to vote for a whole year, unless he is hindered by legitimate motive, verifiable by the Pilier; therefore the custom was introduced whereby the hindered person during the course of the three days submits to the above said Pilier justifications for not being able to be in the Langue. Each Religious must present two notes, in which are given the names of those, whom he judges capable of that office. Who obtains the major number of votes is considered chosen as first Uditore, and with the same proportion of votes the second Uditore, with the usual system that in case of parity of votes, the senior is considered chosen.

The Pilier then gives notice of the nominations to the Ordinary Council, where confirmation is proceeded with, and the elected persons take the oath.

---

[17] *Cons. 22. May 1671.*
[18] *Cons. 15. June 1615, 26. October d.to.*
[19] *6. July 1576.*

The election being in this manner concluded, the new sixteen Uditori assemble at the Treasury and from the first eight, three are chosen, known as Inspectors of Registers (*Ispettori dei libri*); two *Uditori della Camera* (Auditors of the Chamber) and two others Examiners (*Visitatori*). *Ordinaz. 85 del Tesoro* gives minute details as to their respective duties. At this meeting, as everyone notes, the eight substitute Uditori do nothing else other than being present.

The duty of the three Inspectors is to ensure the correctness of the Registers of the Treasury, so that these are kept up to date; and without their previous examination no one has the right to mark any entry therein.

The duty of the two Uditori of the Chamber is to assist in all the meetings of the Ven. Procurators of the Treasury, having however a consultative vote.

To the examining Commissioners is entrusted the duty of verifying all purchases and sales of the effects of the Treasury, of inspecting (according to necessity) the various offices, and of deciding all transactions not exceeding the sum of one thousand *scudi*; however for those exceeding this amount, it is expedient that the Ven. Chamber adds two other Knights.

Chapter XII

Tribunal of Debtors (*Tribunale dei Debitori*)

The Tribunal (known to the public) as that of the Debtors was set up by the last Sacred Chapter General in virtue of *Ordinaz. 13 sotto il titolo della Regola*. It is made up of a Bailiff, a Commandeur with the rank of a Knight, a professed Knight, a Conventual priest and a secular Doctor of Law.

This assembly, however, does not have any ordinary jurisdiction; it was established to prevent, that the Knights and Religious, who are not yet Commandeurs, would burden themselves with debts.

Without the permission given in advance by this Tribunal Knights and other Religious both professed and novices cannot contract debts; and if they contract such debts the obligation is invalid whether it is entered into by private writing or by public deed[20].

This prohibition was enjoined by the present Prince Grandmaster on his subjects by means of an Edict containing the Ordinances cited above[21].

Chapter XIII

Tribunal of Spoils (*Tribunale degli Spogli*)

Two Knights of different nationality and often one of them being a Commandeur, together with a Doctor of Law either Religious or Secular make up this Tribunal.

The history of the setting up of this Tribunal is given in details by Caravita[22].

It is authorized to draw up the process of claims by creditors on spoils of deceased Religious, but it is noted that according to an uninterrupted old custom the Tribunal cannot proceed unless the claim by the creditors is submitted to it by the Ven. Chamber of Accounts (Camera dei Conti).

The cited author asserts that in 1628 the Commissioners of the Spoils together with the then Secretary to the Treasury agreed that the creditors submit in the same terms their request to the Ven. Chamber of Accounts

---

[20] *Ord. 14 della Regola.*
[21] *Pramat. fog. 401.*
[22] *Del Comun. Tesoro cap. 39 n. 1.*

(*Camera dei Conti*) *so as to declare, whether it wants to take cognizance of the credit or credits; if it does not want, the document is referred to the Commissioners of the Spoils, thereby it neither commits nor delegates but remits;* consequently it is understood that after this decree has been emanated the Ven. Chamber of Accounts divests itself of any authority and interference in such a way that, having recoursed the abovementioned Chamber to remove one of the Commissioners, being suspect, the Chamber itself remitted the request to the Grandmaster, and the Sacred Council by Decree of 13. February 1672 considering itself incompetent. Regarding judgements of the priority of creditors proffered by this Tribunal, it is customary that the Chancellor of the Tribunal simply reads the sentence in the abovementioned Chamber.

Chapter XIV

Tribunal of Legitimacy and Nobility

On 11. April 1644 the Sacred Council set up a Tribunal known as that of Legitimacy and Nobility, which was confirmed by the Chapter General of 1777 in virtue of *Ordinaz. 62 del Ricevimento dei Fratelli.*

It is made up of four professed Knights, of different nationality and an Assessor of the rank of Conventual Chaplain.

The first ones are deputized by the Grandmaster and Council, and the Lawyer by the Grandmaster.

It should be properly called an advisory assembly rather than a Tribunal, because it does not have any jurisdiction or judicial power; it is only entrusted to notify the Sacred Ordinary Council of the disputes which arise between the Langues and those aspiring to be received in the three grades of the Sacred Order.

In the cited Ordinance one reads the terms of reference of this assembly. Our laws require the proofs of those to be received in the three grades accepted by the Ven. Langues *nem. discr.* in order to consider the reception completed. Therefore in case that either the proofs had been refused by the Langues or that there were contrary votes regarding same, even in minor number, then this Tribunal proceeds by hearing the parties and then forwards its vote through the Assessor to the Ordinary Council recording in anticipation in its protocols the terms of such examination, for which purpose there is a Secretary.

The second commission is so conceived: *in case of appeal to the Ven. Complete Council to support the opinion given to the Ven. Ordinary Council.* It appears that this expression is meant when the Sacred Ordinary Council has proffered the sentence uniform to the given advice, but if for the sake of example the Conservators opined for the acceptance of the proofs and the Sacred Ordinary Council decreed against, then, against their advice, they must support the sentence, as they must equally so practise in appeals to the Holy See interposed by the pretenders from sentences proffered by the Complete Council.

The expenses incurred for these disputes are provided from funds known as that of the Nobility (*Cassa della Nobilta'*) administered by the Ven. Common Treasury (Comun Tesoro). By way of endowment it was established that who in all the Langues is received in one of the three grades, should pay five *scudi*, in the rank of page of the Grandmaster, ten *scudi* and those with dispensation of minor age (*dispensa della minor eta'*) fifteen *scudi*.

In the three Langues of France and in that of Italy the new families in the Sacred Order, before the compilation of the proofs, in the respective Chapters must submit the documents of primoridial titles, that is to say, the justificative documents of nobility and legitimacy, as one understands in the title of *Ricev. de Fratelli*; hence also in disputes anent their validity and sufficiency are involved as in those of the proofs, the Conservators of Legitimacy and Nobility.

Chapter XV

Provincial Chapters

Outside the Convent and in the Priorates of the realms, where the Sacred Order has its estates, there are two Tribunals: one is called Provincial Chapter and the other Provincial Assembly. *Caravita*[23] remarks that since the Chapters General were instituted for the needs of the whole Order, so the Provincial Chapters were set up for the needs of the Provinces.

The Chapter is made up of the Prior or in his absence his Lieutenant, the Bailiffs known as Capitular, all the Commandeurs, Knights, Conventual Chaplains and Servants-at-arms. The Prior, the Bailiffs and Commandeurs must without fail be present at the Chapters, under pain of paying to the Treasury double Responsion[24]; the others says *Ordin. 20 del Cap.* have to be invited by the Prior, that is to say, they participate if they want.

The Chaplains of Obedience may intervene, however without the faculty of casting their vote in the deliberations[25].

The Provincial Chapters are convened every year from the second Sunday of June up to the 24 of the same month[26]. The meeting lasts three days, which may however be prorogued for another three days, with the plurality of votes[27].

The requisites for casting a vote at the Chapters are those of being professed, having resided three years in the Convent, excepted are the

---

[23] *Comp. Tit. 6. cap. 6.*
[24] *Stat. XIX. del Capit.*
[25] *Ordinaz. 23. Cap.*
[26] *Ordinaz. 18 e 19 detto.*
[27] *Ordinaz. 29 detto.*

Brethren of the Langue of Alemagne[28] and following their example those of the Anglo-Bavarian Langue, not being debtors to the Treasury[29] and belonging to that Priorate, where the Chapter is held. But in the Langues where the Priorates are in common, then every Brother can take part and cast his vote, as is today the case of the Langue of Provence so that consequently the Knight of Toulouse can cast his vote in the Chapter of St. Giles, and the Religious of the latter at the Chapter of Toulouse.

In Italy the same occurs, because, although the Priorates in 1784 were divided by the Conciliating Plan (*Piano Conciliativo*), nothing was mentioned on this matter.

The Capitular Sessions are presided over by the Prior, in his absence by his Lieutenant, and in the absence of the latter by the most senior knight[30] but if there are Bailiffs they precede the Lieutenants, but if they are not Knights Grand Cross *Ordinaz.*[31] stipulates: *"if amongst the capitulars there is a Bailiff, who has an active and a passive vote in the Ven. Council and that the Lieutenant of the Prior is a Knight Little Cross"* would be construed that also to the Bailiffs of Grace is bestowed this precedence.

The procedure therefore, (when in the Chapter there are Capitular Bailiffs or of Grace, and Bailiffs who are Ambassadors at Royal Courts) dictates as follows: if the Lieutenant of the Prior is a Bailiff or Capitular or of Grace or less preeminent than the others, who are present, he precedes everybody else: in his name the Chapter is convened and is entrusted with all matters; in short in everything and for all intents and purposes he has the prerogatives of his principal; if the Lieutenant is Knight Little Cross and there intervenes the Ambassador decorated with

---

[28] *Ordinaz. 22 detto.*
[29] *Stat. XLIV Tesoro.*
[30] *Stat. XII dei Priori Ordinaz. 19 del Cap.*
[31] *Ordinaz. 25 del Capit.*

the Grand Cross, he precedes all the Bailiffs as long as they are pre-eminent and senior, and if this is not the case, the most pre-eminent Bailiff; but in both these instances proposing matters for discussion is always reserved to the Lieutenant.

The Provincial Chapter commences with the celebration of Holy Mass and the reading of the Rule.

The Chapters are vested with both civil and criminal jurisdiction and regular correction over all the Brethren residing within the limits of the Priorate[32] included also the Bailiffs[33], criminal jurisdiction is limited however since it is not empowered to profer sentences with punishment of deprivation of the Habit and of the estates[34].

The Chapter deputizes Commissioners to inspect the improvements of the Dignities, Commanderies and Members, and also appoints Commissioners to compile proofs of those to be received in the three grades, on which proofs the Chapter delivers its deliberations.

The Sagra Ruota Romana in its decision *Melevitana Habitus 28 Gennaro 1686 avanti Albergati* asserted that the deliberations of the Chapters on matters of proofs of Nobility and other requisites of the pretenders were definite sentences; an error, which the Sacred Order could not permit to pass unheeded; therefore it recoursed to the same Tribunal and requested that *ad obviandum praejudicio, quod suis particularibus Legibus, seu Statutis illatum timebat per suppositum in decisione edita, etc.* the devised declaration be reformed; and in fact it emanated the decision entitled *Melevitana Habitus dei 5 Maggio 1688 avanti Emerix* whereby it was established that *Capitulum Provinciale nullam habet auctoritatem judicandi, sed*

---

[32] *Stat. III dei Priori.*
[33] *Ordinaz. 28 del Capitolo.*
[34] *Stat. VII. Dei Priori.*

solum facultatem deputandi Commissarios pro fabricando processu super pro-
bationibus faciendis a petente admitti ad Habitum, illumque fabricatum trans-
mittendi ad Eminentissimum Magnum Magistrum, vel ad Concilium Ordina-
rium: (Here is a slight mistake: the proof is transmitted to the respective
Langue and not to the Grandmaster and Council). Then it passes to define that the deliberation of the Chapter *est votum simpliciter consultivum,*
dum Magnus Magister, & Venerandum Concilium Ordinarium non tenetur
illud sequi, nec ab eo interponitur appellatio; adeoque nomen sententiae non
meretur.

All the deliberations and other provisions must be taken according to
the system of all our Tribunals by secret ballot[35] and the Chapters are
enjoined to transmit to the respective Langues a true copy of the deliberations together with a note of those Bailiffs and Commandeurs who
did not intervene[36].

Chapter XVI

Provincial Assembly

This is an assembly which is held six month following the Provincial
Chapter, that is to say, in November of each year. The Bailiffs and
Commandeurs are not bound to attend. The Prior or his Lieutenant to-
gether with three Religious constitute a quorum. To this Assembly or
Tribunal, it seems, can be applied all that has been said anent the Pro-
vincial Chapter.

---

[35] *Ordinaz. 26 del Capitolo.*
[36] *Ordinaz. 32 e 33 del Capitolo.*

Chapter XVII

Assembly of the Conventual Chaplains

There is in the Convent another inferior Tribunal known as the Assembly of the Conventual Chaplains. The Prior of the Conventual Church of St. John of the Sacred Order is its Head and President. The Conventual priests of all the Langues form this body. The priesthood is the only requisite necessary to be admitted in the Assembly and cast the vote.

As regards the manner of convening the Assembly there is specific legislation[37] which lays down that when it is a matter of receiving Conventual Chaplains or other similar matters, it is necessary to obtain the Grandmaster's permission; but when it meets to deal with the administration of its property and to appoint its officials, then the permission beformentioned is not required. However the Langues have to be notified in advance of the agenda.

In virtue of *Ordinaz. 1 dei Prior* this Tribunal is empowered to punish priests, deacons, subdeacons and clerics queried either by the Prior or by the Vice Prior *for not attending* (these are the words of the Law) *divine Service* (Divini Uffiçj) *or other kind of crime committed against the good and ancient customs or not having obeyed the precepts of the said Prior and Vice Prior or anything else which they will have done that may deserve punishment.* It will be noted from these expressions that the Ven. Assembly is the Tribunal which has the exclusive jurisdiction of punishing the faults and crimes relating to church service and disobedience to the precepts of the Prior and Vice Prior. Consequently it is a positive violation of the Law to recourse to others in such cases.

The Prior as Head has the right to propose matters for discussion and nominations of the Procurators and other Officials of the Ven. Assembly,

---

[37] *Ordinaz. 6 del Maestro.*

subject however to the judgement of the Assembly by the usual means of balloting[38].

The said Ven. Assembly is empowered to adjudicate the pretenders to be received in the grade of Conventual Chaplains within the requisites of the letters and of the ecclesiastical side. On other occasions the Assembly pretended that following its refusal there should be no appeal, but this was excluded by the Sagra Ruota Romana[39]. Hence in such instances appeal is referred to the Sacred Ordinary Council, where Commissioners are deputized for examining the merits of the letters submitted by the pretender and for the ecclesiastical side. In this type of lawsuits, though related to receptions, the Tribunal of Legitimacy and Nobility should not be involved.

Chapter XVIII

The Jurisdiction of a Judge in our Tribunals of First Instance

Although in *Stat. V del Consiglio* it is strictly prescribed that in disputes between Brethren these may be proceeded with summarily *more militari* without papers, but only that the pleaders on their part allege verbally their reasons and that solely on the basis of their verbal statements (*nude parole*, says the text) judgement may be delivered (*si distribuisca la giustizia*). However necessity required that one may avail oneself of an attorney, provided he belongs to the Sacred Order and state his own reasons in writing[40].

In lawsuits anent Commanderies, Bailiwicks, Priorates and Elections to Conventual Dignities, of which, as is stipulated[41] the Ordinary Council acts as judge at first instance, the plaintiff is the candidate less senior,

---

[38] *Ordinaz. 2 dei Priori.*
[39] *Melevit. Habitus 1. Luglio 1718 avanti Lancet.*
[40] *Ordinaz. 11 del Consiglio.*
[41] *Cap. VII. di questo libro.*

called *fiernaldo* and the summoned accused is the senior. After the submissions will have been made by the competitors to the respective Ven. Langues and there will be the generic re-instatement by the same Langues in favour of the capable senior, the *fiernaldo* within the term of eight effective days running from the day of re-instatement must submit the motives, whereby he proves the senior incapable by means of a note couched as follows:

"Before me Bailiff NN Vice-Chancellor appeared NN stating that on etc. he requested the Ven. Langue NN the Commandery or Bailliwick or Priorate or Conventual Dignity NN in case of incapacity of Commandeur NN. In fulfilment as to what is prescribed by *Ordinaz. 3 sotto il titolo delle Commende* alleges Commandeur NN to be incapable (here are specified the motives) and etc".

Within the month after the said eight effective days the said *fiernaldo* has to lodge with the Castellania this other note:

"Before me Bailiff NN Vice-Chancellor appeared Commandeur NN to declare that he intends to move the dispute anent Commandery NN against Commandeur NN before the Sacred Ordinary Council etc".

Then in the course of four other months the *fiernaldo* must introduce the lawsuit by making four summons known to us as Commandments through the Master-Equerry to the senior. The form is as follows:

"Master-Equerry, by permission of His Most Eminent Highness at the instance of NN issue four summons to NN to the effect that wishing to oppose the request which the pretender intends to make, to be sent to him the Bulls of the Commandery NN or of being elected Conventual Bailiff NN, or of being promoted to Priorate or Bailiwick NN appears before the Sacred Ordinary Council to be fixed by His Most Eminent Highness, etc. Subsequently you will refer in the opportune place and at the opportune time".

One notes however that these summons may be made verbally by the Master-Equerry, and not in writing, whilst in lawsuits *more Militari* such as ours the Sagra Ruota Romana defined[42] *quod non est necessaria citatio in scriptis etc. sed sufficit quod intervenerit certioratio.*

---

[42] *Decis. 716. n. 2. part. 2 dei Recenz.*

After all these formalities the litigating parties must present to the Vice-Chancellor the decree of their respective reasons[43].

The Council being convened the Vice-Chancellor on instructions by the Grandmaster starts the hearing of the lawsuit. Therefore the advocates of the parties submit their case (if the Grandmaster so permits) or their written submissions are read out.

Having in this manner heard the contenders all those who are not members of the Council withdraw and behind closed doors the Vice-Chancellor explains in brief the merit of the dispute, repeating all the respective reasons of both parties, and hence one proceeds with the scrutiny of ballots for the decision.

Often it so happens the Council decides on deputizing Commissioners; then the Grandmaster and in his absence the President appoints six of two different Langues from those of the pleaders but of the same rank; their names and surnames written on small ballot papers two of them are drawn[44] to whom is entrusted the hearing of the lawsuit and to give their advice, with authority to solve all the incidents which may arise[45].

When in the Council there arises a discrepancy on the wording, whether Commissioners should be deputized or the lawsuit decided; Caravita hints[46], that a vote ought to be taken in such circumstance, because it may well happen that who had the least number of votes may win the case, and he argues as follows; "if two Brethren compete for a Commandery, wanting to take a vote on the wording and on the merit of the case, then it would be convenient to give one for the collation of the Commandery to the senior, one to the *fiernaldo* and the third to the deputation of the Commissioners. The Councillors being thirty, if ten are

---

[43] *Stat. 12 del Cons.*
[44] *Ordinaz. 13 del Cons.*
[45] *Stat. 16 del Cons.*
[46] *Comp. Tit. 7 cap. 6.*

for the senior, twelve for the *fiernaldo* and eight for the deputation of the Commissioners, thus as a result the monstruosity that who had the least number of votes remains the winner".

The deputized Commissioners in case of slow progress by one of the parties for making its submissions have the right to impose a time limit as they think proper and under threat that in case of contumacy they will proceed with the drawing up of their advice[47].

The Commissioners may avail themselves of a consultant acceptable to them, with authority to keep him in secret to the parties[48].

In case that either one or both of them cannot continue as Commissioners either because they are legitimately hindered to continue in that office or because they are removed as suspects, the Grandmaster himself on his own authority, without the need for the parties to convoke the Council, has the power to subrogate[49].

The Commissioners after having heard all the information, draw up the report and duly signed by them it is submitted to the Grandmaster for its being then forwarded to the Council.

Before this new proposition the new summons must be done of the same tune as the first ones and the advocates must either verbally or in writing repeat their information.

In lawsuits wherein there is contradiction of proofs between the pretenders and the respective Langues, this other method is followed:
The pretender, who considers himself aggravated either by the refusal of his primordial titles in the Langues where this formality is practised or of his proofs, does not produce a formal appeal, since the delib-

---

[47] *Ordinaz. 20 del. Cons.*
[48] *Ordinaz. 14 del Cons.*
[49] *Ordinaz. 18 del Cons.*

erations of the Langues are not sentences, but submits in the Chancery a note couched in these terms:

Before me Bailiff NN Vice-Chancellor has appeared NN as attorney of the Noble NN pretending to be received in the dignity of NN of the Ven. Langue NN submitting, that the Langue by its deliberation of etc. rejected with the plurality of votes (either the Primordial titles or the proofs of his principal) against the dictates of justice, therefore so that silence may not be of prejudice to him, protests of being very aggravated and therefore intends to bring his complaints to His Most Eminent Highness and to the Sacred Council etc.

Then on the part of the pretender a verbal request is made to the Procurators of the contradicting Langue to remit either the documents of the primodial titles or the proofs (processo delle prove) to the senior commissioner of the Conservators of the Legitimacy and Nobility, who in terms of *Ordinaz. 62 del Ricev. o de'Fratelli* must deal with the matter forthwith.

It is the practice that the *processo* or the file is seen round by all the commissioners and the Assessor; when these are informed, the senior fixes the day, on which the parties are heard and consequently the following summon is issued:

"Master-Equerry, at the instance of NN as attorney of the Noble NN notify the knights NN as Procurators of the Ven. Langue N that at etc. on the day etc. a meeting will be held of the Tribunal of Legitimacy and Nobility to hear the submissions on the *Processo* (proofs) or on the Primordial titles of the Noble NN his principal; therefore you will solicit them to appear at the place where the said Tribunal is usually convened at the time indicated etc".

Finally on the part of the pretender four summons are issued to the Procurators of the contradicting Langue "Master Equerry, by permission of His Most Eminent Highness at the instance of NN as Procurator etc. issue the four summons to NN Procurators of the Ven. Langue N to the effect that wishing to oppose the request which he intends to make so that either the proofs or the primordial titles of the Noble his principal may be accepted as good and valid, appear before the first Sacred Ordinary Council on etc. to be fixed by His Most Eminent Highness etc.

On the day of the proposition of the lawsuit in Council after either the contradictory of the advocates or the reading of the memos, the Assessor verbally declares the opinion of the commissioners and then within closed doors the decision is made by secret ballot.

The same procedure is adopted when the proofs or primordial titles will be contradicted in the Langue by the minority of votes even if by only one vote, with the only difference that the summon to appear is affixed on the door of the Magistral Palace and on that of the Auberge of the respective Langue, worded as follows:

"Master Equerry, at the instance of NN as attorney of NN you will give notice in the usual public places that on the day etc. - the Tribunal of Legitimacy and Nobility will meet to examine the proofs or the primordial titles of the Noble his principal, to the effect that who wishes to give exception may appear in the place where *usually the Tribunal meets* on the day and at the hour indicated etc. of subsequent meetings you may refer in the opportune place and at the opportune time, and the public summons in the following terms":

"Master Equerry, by permission of His Most Eminent Highness at the instance of NN as attorney of the Noble NN you will issue the public summons in the usual places to the effect that should there be anyone who wishes to oppose to the request which he intends to prove as being good and valid either the proofs or the primordial titles of the Noble his principal, may appear before the first Sacred Ordinary Council on the day to be fixed by His Most Eminent Highness etc".

When the Sacred Council has proffered the sentences, these are read in public, which publication means the notification of the sentence which in secular Tribunals the winner makes to the loser.

In the Camera dei Conti (Chamber of Accounts) the procedure follows the same system of *more militari* at least nowadays: the plaintiffs against the Treasury through the aegis of the Secretary present to the Tribunal their petitions supported by the relative documents, equivalent to libel of the legal profession and to the summon.

When it is a matter of pretensions of some importance and it is not possible to give a decision forthwith, commissioners are deputized. And they are appointed by the Grand Commendator, if he is present, otherwise by the Grand Cross, most pre-eminent among the Procurators of the Treasury and the Procurator of the Grandmaster.

Before the commissioners if the plaintiff is a person of the Sacred Order, the defence for the Treasury is entrusted to the Procurator of religious lawsuits (*Procuratore delle Cause Religioso*), if he is a laymen the defence is entrusted to the Procurator of the secular lawsuits (*Procuratore delle Cause Secolare*).

Then when it is a matter of minor claims, which do not merit to burden the parties with expenses, it is referred for examination to the Procurators of Lawsuits who will then give their advice.

Having heard the reports either of the Commissioners or of the Procurators of Lawsuits, sentence is pronounced in the following laconic form = either there is no case or we adhere to the report of the Commissioners or to the report of the Procurators of Lawsuits, Advocate NN.

No vote is taken unless there is a discrepancy of opinions among the judges, who fail to reach agreement.

Chapter XIX

Appeals

From sentences proffered by the Ordinary Council one may appeal to the Sacred Complete Council[50]. And this within the term of ten days running from the day sentence is proffered[51] consecutively, that is to say, all the subsequent days including feast days *in honorem Dei*. The form usually is worded as follows:

"Before me Bailiff Vice-Chancellor NN appeared NN who feeling himself very aggravated by the sentence proffered by the Sacred Ordinary Council in the current lawsuit between him and NN has appealed and appeals to His Most Eminent Highness and to the Sacred Complete Council etc".

Within four months appellant should introduce the lawsuit in the Sacred Complete Council from the day of appeal, in which four month are not included the canicular holidays which commence on 29. June and end on 29. September[52]. However it is understood that the person against whom appeal is being made can anticipate the appellant[53] which introduction is considered executed by submitting summons, that is, the four summons in the following terms: "Master Equerry - by permission of His Most Eminent Highness at the instance of NN issue four summons to NN to the effect that wishing to oppose the request which he intends submitting to revoke the sentence proffered against him by the Sacred Ordinary Council on etc. he may appear before the Sacred Complete Council to be fixed by His Most Eminent Highness etc".

From sentences of the Chamber of Accounts (Camera dei Conti) and of the Commissioners deputized by the Grandmaster appeal is interposed to the Ordinary Council, and this like all the others within the term of

---

[50] *Stat. XIX del Cons.*
[51] *Stat. XVIII eodem.*
[52] *Ordinaz. 50 del Cons.*
[53] *Ordinaz. 29 del Cons.*

ten days and with the obligation on the part of the appellant to continue in the course of four month[54] otherwise the sentence is referred for judgement.

One would note that from sentences of the Camera dei Conti against the administrators of effects and property of the Treasury no suspensory appeal is admitted, but the condemned must pay before being heard by the Ordinary Council[55].

The Commissioners deputized by the Council always have the power as before mentioned, to decide all incidents and emerging matters; and whenever one of the parties feels aggrieved by these interlocutory sentences, appeal is referred to the Council which deputized the Commissioners, but has to interpose either on the same day or on the following[56] - as is also stated in the Statute[57] - must be dealt with and finalized (*seguitata e terminata*) *within ten days from the day it is interposed*. For the term *seguitata* most appropriately means that if the appellant is negligent, the decree is referred for judgement; but *terminata* at the most should mean, that the appellant must make request for proposition in the Council. But if it is futile, then, most obviously, he must not be prejudiced.

From the sentences of Priors and of the Provincial Assemblies (*Assemblee Provinciali*) in disputes anent their jurisdiction, appeal is made to the Provincial Chapter (*Capitolo Provinciale*); from sentences of this Tribunal to the Ordinary Council, and thence to the Complete Council, with the obligation of introducing the lawsuit within the term of one year which may be prorogued for another year for a legitimate cause[58].

---

[54] *Ordinaz. 44. Tesoro, Ordinaz. 28 Cons.*
[55] *Stat. XLVIII, ed Ordinaz. 44 Tesoro.*
[56] *Stat. XVIII del Cons.*
[57] *Stat. XX eodem.*
[58] *Stat. XX del Cons.*

The Chaplains of Obedience (Cappellani d'Ubbidienza) attached to the service of the Priorates, Bailiwicks and Commanderies in case of grievances received from their principals are at liberty to appeal to the Provincial Chapter. The context of the Statute[59] indicates, that they can however even bring their claim before the Ordinary Council.

In the *Statuto XVI del Consiglio* it is prohibited to appeal from decrees delivered by the Sacred Chapter General (Sagro Capitolo Generale), being the supreme of our Tribunals; from the creation of officials, from declarations of the Statutes and Ordinances, which the Sacred Ordinary Council has the power to promulgate, from executive mandates and from interlocutories on the suspicion of the Councillors of the two Councils, from sentences of the Provincial Chapters pronounced in litigations between Religious in pretensions not exceeding the sum of hundred scudi.

Finally appeal from elections of Commandeurs and Brethren to Bailiffs Grand Cross is prohibited, adding: *"one may appeal nevertheless from promotions, that is, from the translation of Bailiffs to other Dignities"*. It is good to know, that the Conventual Bailiffs, that is, the eight Piliers are elected by the Ordinary Council, and being elected as such they have the *Jusque-sito* to Capitular Dignitaries, that is, Priorates and Bailiwicks of their respective Langues. When it concerns their election there is no case for appeal whatsoever; the Council, after having decided, invests the chosen person with the Dignity and he enters thereby in the exercise and in the expensive maintenance of the Auberge. When then it is a question of promotion of the Conventual Bailiff to Capitular Dignities, then the lawsuit is considered as ordinary and suspensive appeals are admitted. The motive of such provision must be, that our legislators considered it to be dangerous for the good government of the Sacred Order, that the Langues should remain without a chief for a long time, as they would have remained had appeals been allowed. On the contrary then, since there is

---

[59] *Stat. XVII del Cons.*

no great harm, in fact none, that for some years the Priorates and Baili-wicks may remain vacant, appeal was allowed.

Here is a query which requires a solution: sometimes and not infre-quent, it happens that the Pilier, that is, Conventual Bailiff opts for a Bailiwick or Priorate, in such a manner that such Bailiwick or Priorate is contended by more knights, who as senior and who in case of incapacity of such Pilier lands the dispute in the Sacred Ordinary Council. It is doubtful if from the sentence, which is proffered in this lawsuit, there is suspensive appeal. In the cited regulative Ordinance of appeal it seems that particular significance is given to the terms "Election and Promotion (*Elezione e Promozione*)". By election one understands, when a Knight Lit-tle Cross is elected Bailiff; by promotion one understands the option from one dignity to another. If this explanation is correct, the doubt is quickly removed. In the case proposed with the sentence an election is held, therefore there is no place for suspensive appeal.

Two conforming sentences of the Ordinary and Complete Councils con-stitute according to our laws matter as adjudicated.

The Bull *Inter Illustria* of Benedict XIV is the legislation now in force re-garding this matter[60] couched as follows: "We establish and decree that no appeal is admitted and conceded in suspensive from a sentence given by the Judge of second instance; when however the said second sentence is not destructive of the first already definitive or given in such a man-ner, that it has effect of truly definitive, and destructing the first only in some part, the second cannot change and be made valid in such matter; but where two sentences wholly conform between them, they are equal to three and render the lawsuit decided and constitute the matter adjudicated".

"Therefore it can be put into execution immediately by the party who has won such sentence. If the losing party has neither despatched nor

---

[60] Para. *20*

legitimately submitted to the winning party within the space of the next three months the usual special summon to the Papal Adviser (Uditore Pontificio), at that time in office, he will not have obtained from him the suspension of the execution".

Therefore on the lapse of three months, the party which had obtained the two sentences makes recourse to the Ordinary Council by means of summons to his adversary, requesting that appeal be declared abandoned and judgement be carried into effect.

All this however takes place when the conforming sentences are two; but when they are three of our Tribunals, then re-judgement is constituted notwithstanding any appeal to the Holy See, as happens in lawsuits moved in first instance in the Provincial Chapters or in the Camera dei Conti, then for first appeal in the Ordinary Council, and for third appeal in the Complete Council (Consiglio Compito).

Chapter XX

Public Audience

A very old custom introduced the mixed Tribunal, called the Public Audience, in order to decide lawsuits between Religious and Laymen. Since two or more centuries it takes cognizance of appeal from sentences of the Chamber of Accounts (Camera dei Conti) delivered in lawsuits between the Treasury and laymen, from the Tribunal of the Spoils, from the Tribunal of Armaments, from the Tribunal of Houses and from sentences of Commissioners deputized by the Grandmaster and today from the new Tribunal of Debtors (Tribunale dei Debitori) given however, as one would anticipate, when lawsuits arise between Laymen and Religious.

The members of this Tribunal are all those forming the Sacred Ordinary Council, the Castellan and civil Judge of the Castellania, the Captain of the Rod (Capitano della Verga) and the civil Judge of the city of Notabile (Mdina) and the new Magistrate of Justice.

Chapter XXI

The Grandmaster

In Chapter 4 of this work it was stated that executive power was entrusted to the Sacred Order on the principles of the monarchical system. Here is the proof.

According to our laws the Grandmaster was constituted the highest superior within the Sacred Order[61]. It was fundamental law that prescribed to all the Religious, both individuals and united in various bodies, the most immediate and exact obedience to his commands[62]; commands which are just and honest, that is to say, meant for the preservation and prosperity of the Order[63].

In order to prevent the easy passage to despotism from such supreme authority, especially over persons to whom obedience is not a simple virtue, but solemn vow, it was necessary to set up an intermediary Tribunal to guard the limits of such authority.

This Tribunal is known as Sguardio dei Fratelli (Protection of the Brethren) in *Statuti XII, and XIII della Regola* one reads the sage legislation conceived in the following precise words: "The Rule requires that the Brother obeys his Master in everything he shall command, whereby the Rule excludes nothing whatsoever; nevertheless it is understood that it has its limits etc. Whence it has been determined, that when the Superior

---

[61] *Stat. VI della Regola.*
[62] *Stat. VII eod.*
[63] *Stat. VII della Regola.*

issues an order which does not conform to the Statutes, Usages, Customs of the Religion, the Brother must seek the protection of the Brethren (Sguardio dei Fratelli), because our obedience is not meant to be otherwise and we ought not to be forced for the sake of obedience if not in so far as the Rule and our good customs ordain, which our Superior has promised to observe, and if He acts against the oath the Brother is not bound to obey him".

And since the request for protection should without fail be submitted to the Grandmaster, if He refuses it, the Brother must continue to ask for convocation, and *in the meantime*, the text reads, *the Brother is not bound to obey the command, until protection has been recognized and adjudicated.*

Of the ensuing dispute as to whether the case merits the convocation of the Sguardio, the competent Judge is the Complete Council (Consigilio Compito)[64].

Of this Tribunal we have a particular section in our Code and it is the eighth section. But since in civil matters, when the Sacred Order established itself in Malta, it remained in disuse, and today it is the Tribunal in Criminal lawsuits; we shall discuss this when commenting on Prohibitions and Penalties (Proibizioni e Pene).

One reads about all the Preeminences, Prerogatives and Magistral Collations in the Catalogue of the alphabetical compendium of the Statutes compiled with the most accurate precision published by the Uditore (Adviser) to His Most Eminent Highness and most worthy Secretary of the Chancery Commendatore Fra Gaetano Bruno and each item is discussed in the respective sections.

---

[64] *Stat. X dello Sguardio.*

Book Two

Chapter I

The Rule

In other Religions and Orders by Rule (Regola) one understands the List (Catalogo) of the various duties described by Suarez[65]. In the Sacred Order of Jerusalem this term means the contents of *Statuto I di questo titolo*, that is to say, the three solemn vows of Chastity, Poverty and Obedience.

Our provident legislators for conscience's sake declared by *Stat. XXV* under this title that transgression of the Rule binds the soul and the body; however the contraventions of the Statutes and other Laws bind only the body, that is, transgressers of the laws do not commit mortal sin but are only punishable with temporal penance, inflicted by the same laws. However it is understood by the cited law that: *omission or transgression of any of them does not bind the soul according to divine Law and Canon Statutes.*

Some moralists considered the distinct declaration to be erroneous for the following reason: in every statute, they argue, one reads the terms: *we decree, we ordain et similia*, being indicative, as everyone knows, of the positive intention of the Superior of being obeyed; the vow of obedience binds the soul, therefore the transgression of *the statutes does not bind only the body but also the soul.*

The reply is very simple: according to all theologians it is an irrefutable principle, as Suarez assures as per text cited above[66], that when in any Order or Religion those vested with legislative power declared, as is the case with Ours, that the violation of the laws decreed by them binds

---

[65] *De Relig. tom. 4. lib. 8. cap. 1, 2, 3.*
[66] *Tract. De Relig. tom. 4. lib. 8. n. 2 & 3.*

only the body, therefore correspondingly to this prevention must be understood the terms: *we decree, we ordain et simlia*. The mentioned author indeed adds, that when in the disposition are added the words *in virtue of holy obedience* (in virtu' di santa Ubbidienza), as, for example, in *Stat XXIV* of this title, then it is understood that the legislators have wanted to constitute the fact prescribed by them within the limits of proper and rigorous obedience. Consequently the transgressor sins against this his vow, and therefore binds the soul.

Only these three vows are professed in the Sacred Order. Villagut[67] is completely wrong when he says that we have the fourth vow to defend by the sword and the danger of the Christians' life from the infidels.

Chapter II

Obedience

Every Religious of whatsoever dignity, rank and condition must obey the Grandmaster *Stat VI* of this title with the modification however of the ensuing *Stat XII*, the contents of which have been dealt with in the Chapter of the preceding book.

The Knights and Servants-at-arms must obey the Marshal; on this matter we have *Stat VIII and Stat IX*. In the first one there is the abovementioned general conclusion which seems to impose obedience to the Marshal on all occasions. The second Statute demands the obedience of the Knights and Servants-at-arms in the exercise of arms. Indeed expressly excepted are the Conventual Bailiffs, their Lieutenants, the Priors, the Castellan d'Emposta, the Capitular Bailiffs and the companions (compagni) of the Grandmaster; I belief in such exemption are also included the Bailiffs *ad honores*.

---

[67] *Decis. 34 n. 5.*

But this prerogative of the Marshal totally ceases when there is present the Grandmaster or his Lieutenant, whilst in the second part of the cited *Statute IX* it is laid down that when the Grandmaster is present, the Marshal and all the others must obey him or his lieutenant.

In the *Stat. I dei Priori* the following is the legislation that we have anent obedience to the Prior of the major Conventual church by the chaplains and conventual clerics.

It commences by stipulating that the said chaplains and clerics come under the commands of the Prior; excepted are the four chaplains of the Grandmaster.

Then it proceeds to enumerate the matters on which these orders may be imposed. These are the punctual celebration of the Ufficj (offices) in the Conventual church, the hearing of confessions, and the administering the sacrament of the Holy Eucharist.

Against the disobedient are inflicted penalties and the procedure is prescribed in *Stat VII della Regola.*

The Brother in the Convent disobeying at the first precept of the Grandmaster or other superior is punished with the penance of the Settena (seven days); at the second precept, with the penance of the Quarantena (40 days); and at the third precept he is deprived of the Habit. Here it would be added that these penalties of Settene and Quarantene were abolished by *Ordinaz. 29 delle Probizioni e Pene*; they were substituted by carceration in the Castle [of St. Angelo]. Nevertheless the guilty of first disobedience must be condemned to imprisonment in the Castle for a month; for the second refusal, for six months.

However before proceeding with the infliction of the said penalties the cited Statute requires that *"for each command not fulfilled, one is accused"* in such a manner that after having intimated the order and justified the will of not obeying, accusation must be brought to the superiors.

This same method is laid down in the cited Statute against the disobedient in the Priorates outside the Convent, with the exception of the privation of the Habit, which is reserved to the Grandmaster and to the Convent. Whence in circumstances of contumacy to the order which is repeated thrice. Trial must be remitted to the Grandmaster and Council.

The disobeying Brother who is residing outside the Convent at the first command of the Grandmaster and Council, if he does not, within the term of nine months, justify the legitimate motives that have either hindered him or delayed the execution, proved of disobedience, without further summon or formality must be condemned to the privation of the Habit - cited *Statute VII* of this title stipulates this.

The Brethren residing outside the Convent must carry out the orders of the Grandmaster and Council, and their decrees with the most scrupulous exactness. The penalties of the transgressors are the following as expressed in the said *Statuto VII*. The Priors disobeying for the first time lose the dividends of one year of one of the Camere Priorali; at the second disobedience, the dividends of two years, and at the third time, of the privation in perpetuity of the same Camera Priorale, and persisting in their contumacy they must be deprived of the Priorate and of all administration.

Bailiffs and Commandeurs disobeyinging for the first time lose one third of the dividends of one year of the Bailiwick or Commandery. Disobeying for the second time, two thirds; for the third time, all the profits of the Commandery in favour of the Common Treasury, and for the fourth time, the Commandery itself, subsequently to be provided for according to the rules of the Sacred Order.

Then the ordinary Religious for the first negligence must be punished by losing one year of seniority, for the second negligence, two years; for the third, three years, and for further negligence total seniority, both that already acquired and that to be acquired.

Chapter III

Chastity

The vow of Religious Chastity, precisely that made by us, is defined by moralists and especially by Bordon[68] in these terms: "*Est promissio Deo facta abstinendi se ab omni actu venereo, mente & opere, sive licito, ut in conjugio, sive illicito, iu extra illud, non solum seminis iffusione, sed etiam, a turpi cogitatione,a delectatione morosa, ab illicito tactu, a turpi aspectu, & hujus generis, per qua castitas, & continentia violatur*".

By this definition every doubt is most easily eliminated, which in such a delicate matter, may occur. Hence I have considered it futile to examine all the questions, which the Casuists promote.

For the strict observance of this vow our legislators are most jealous: by *Statuto V of this title* they have burdened the conscience of the Grandmaster, and what is more remarkable, of every Councillor to watch in this regard over the conduct of the Religious; hence they deputized as perpetual commissioner the Prior of the Major Conventual Church, by ordering that every year two venerable colleagues be appointed to assist him; these were enjoined to find out, whether there is any Religious who may be living miserably in concubinage and having found him they secretly report him to the Superior.

Against the concubinaries *Stat. III of this title* laid down the privation of the commanderies and other property of the Sacred Order, and not having found the guilty of such crime they impose the loss of seniority and besides the privation of the Habit.

In this Statute of no effect today is the disposition that if those deprived of the Habit for this crime be reinstated may remain incapable for a decade from receiving property of the Order, because in virtue of the last

---

[68] *Tratt. de Profes. Regul. cap. 25, n. 2.*

Sacred Chapter General of 1777 by *Stat. XXVII delle Probizioni e Pene* to whatsoever authority was prohibited the restitution of the Habit for those who have been once deprived of it.

The procedure which was laid down by the cited Statute for inflicting punishment for such types of criminals is very cautious: first of all the truth must be ascertained that the Religious may be living in concubinage either by depositions of witnesses worthy of being believed, that is, of the number and quality which Common Law (Dritto Comune) requires, since one may be slandered, or by the confession of the accused. Hence it is prescribed that the concubinary convinced and confessed be warned thrice by the superior to reform himself. If within the term of forty days, running from the day of first warning, the person does not reform but persists in his sacrilegious practice, having used this paternal diligence, the described penalties are inflicted.

According to *Statuto IV of this title* public concubinary is he who publicly supports children, acknowledging them as his own by giving them his surname.

As well as he who keeps in his own house women, of whom the public is scandalized.

On this subject the manner of thinking of our legislators is so delicate that by *Ordinaz. 1. of this title* prohibited Religious from keeping in their houses women younger than fifty years.

Card. Petra nel Commentar alle Costit. Appost. Tom. 2.n.14. fol 29 argues, if the professed knight of Malta can adopt or claim some one as his son, he concludes with good reasons, it is not allowed to him, amongst others, that one of the principal requisites of adoption is that it is *sui juris* who wants to adopt. A circumstance which the Religious of Malta does not have, in view of the vows *alieni juris*.

Chapter IV

The Vow of Poverty

The origin of the Vow of Poverty (Voto di Povertà) which is professed in all religious societies, is assigned by moralists according to the advice of Jesus Christ as recorded in the Gospel of St. Matthew[69] *"Si vis perfectus esse, vade, vende, qua habes, & da pauperibus"* On this score St. Augustine teaches:[70] *"Divinae Scripturae non solum praecepta continent, sed etiam vitam, moresque Sanctorum, ut si forte occultum est, quermadmodum accipiendum sit, quod praecipitur, vel consulitur, in factis justorum intelligatur".* By such guidance in order to have a clear intelligence of the transcribed advice *"Si vis perfectus esse, etc."* means, they add, to lead a system of life held by the Apostles and the first Christians.

This method is described by St. Luke[71]: *"omnes etiam, qui credebant, erant pariter, & habebant omnia communia possessiones, & substantias & vendebant, & dividebant illa omnibus, prout cuique opus erat. Multitudinis autem credentium erat cor unum, & anima una; nec quisquam eorum, qua possidebat, aliquid suum esse dicebat, sed erant illis omnia communia. Neque enim quisquam egens erit inter illos: quotquot enim possessores agrorum, aut domorum erant, vendentes afferebant pretia eorum, quae vendebant, & ponebant ante pedes Apostolorum; dividebatur autem singulis, prout cuique opus erat".*

Chapter V

Nature of the Vow of Poverty

From the text cited from the Acts of the Apostles it results that every individual by joining the society is giving and waiving in favour of that society all and wholly his property. The administration was committed

---

[69] *Cap. XIX*
[70] *De mendac. cap. 15.*
[71] *Act. cap. 3 & 4.*

to certain ministers, who had the duty of providing to everyone the necessities, lodging and clothing. Thus today the vow of Poverty which is professed, is such (tale quale) as that of the Apostles, the divine Counsel was converted into precept.

Chapter VI

Consequence

The truth of the preceding chapter indicates to us that the vow of Poverty contains two deeds: the first one is that the Religious denudes himself in favour of the Religion of all property present and future; the other one is that the Religion takes upon itself to provide the Religious with subsistence and clothing.

Therefore the more or less rigour for the observance of the vow of Poverty depends on the economic system that the Religious society maintains in providing sustenance for its Religious.

The economic system of our Sacred Order one can frankly say is nil by title of sustenance to its individuals. Whilst to those absent from the Convent also for its service, it provides nothing, and to those present so little, which is next to nothing.

In compensation however it left and leaves to the Religious the full usufruct and enjoyment of annuities for life of all their acquests.

These principles produce the following conclusions:

1st That with the vow of Poverty in virtue of the first abdication of every property, which the Religious makes, the Religion acquires for itself the full ownership of all the property present and future of the professed.

2nd. That in the same act of profession, the Religion cedes to the professed the usufruct and use of the latter's property present and future to provide from the same for his sustenance.

3rd. That on the conscience of the same Religious the Sacred Order judges on the quantity for his sustenance.

This liquidation appears difficult to some. I should believe that the conduct on the principles of a good father of the family would be the most secure, which means making all the necessary expenses, useful and modest whilst preserving the rest to his heir.

Chapter VII

Prior Caravita's Opinion

This our accredited author in his compendium gives many counsels to our Religious and I produce them verbatim (tali quali) so that everyone by examining them may regulate one's conscience.

"The proper maintenance of our Brethren includes all that which concerns their status of Religious at the same time being nobles and leading a secular life. *S. Rot coram Caccia Lithuana donation. 5. Maji 1688* which better declares, I say, that under this name everything is included, which is essential for the maintenance of the person, status and family of the Brethren according to their condition, more or less, noble or rich; according to the dignity, they hold within the Religion, or of simple Brethren or of Commandeurs or of Grand Cross; according to the post, they sustain, both in the service of the Religion and of ambassadors and similar posts, as of other princes. And finally according to the quality and custom of the country in which they live".

"The proper maintenance of our Brethren does not consist in an indivisible point, but receives more ranks: the highest, the intermediate and the lowest rank. They will be allowed to avail themselves of the highest, putting aside the intermediate and the lowest rank. *Ex Molin. De Suptit. Disput. 145 & Castropal. Tract. 6. disput. 2 punct. 5 n. 8. in simili de Cleric. Benefic.* And thus the lowest rank being eight hundred *scudi* for the sustenance of a Brother; nine hundred *scudi* for the intermediate dignity, and one thousand *scudi* for the highest; he can spend one thousand *scudi* putting aside the intermediate and the lowest dignity".

"The proper maintenance does not forbid our Brethren from spending some moderate sum for game, hunting and other similar equestrian exercises because although they are indeed Religious, they retain nonetheless the rank of their nobility; and their purpose is not to profess a rigorous observance, but to dedicate their life fighting for Christ *Lezan quaest. Regul. tom. 1. part. 1. cap. 5. n. 18. Pellizzar. Manual. Regul. Tract. 4. cap. 1. n. 178"*.

"The proper maintenance of our Brethren does not exclude moderate and honest feasts and amusements with friends and others *Ex div. Thom Quodlib. 6. art. 12. in simili de Cleric. Benefic.* competing for a reasonable cause, so that it is equally permitted to them to have at their table other Brethren for reason of friendship, of gratitude and other similar motives, always excluded, however, that vain pomp and ostentation which is not without some blame in secular persons".

"The proper maintenance of our Brethren admits and with much liberality the usage of pious works and particularly of hospitality and of charity *Stat. 1, XXVII. Ospit. Stat. VII. Visit e Stat. II. Regol.,* therefore it is allowed to them to support poor parents and more generously than others, because we are more bound towards ours than to strangers *Sanch Cons. lib. 2. cap. 2. dub. 38. n. 5.* And the Sagra Rota *coram Gregor. decis. 401. n. 9* said that the Regular Bishops not only can but must favour their poor nephews. And Bossio *de Dot cap.5. n. 90.* affirms that our Brethren are bound to maintain and favour the poor sisters who cannot otherwise provide for their maintenance and endowment. And not only by revenue accruing from patrimonial property but also that accruing from the commanderies. All this is intended to be practised with due moderation and in so far it is sufficient to maintain them decently in their status, and not with the sole aim of enriching them and enlarging their property. But as regards the use of pious works, our Brethren point out, that according to the doctrine of Navarro *Comment 3 de Regul. n. 7,* and of

Suarez *de Relig. tom. 4, lib. 2. cap. 26. n. 13,* enlarging or improving the monastery for habitation or divine cult or as regards revenue, is a deed more gratifying to God, than supporting the poor in their common needs. Therefore in this case a surer counsel would be the moderation of pious works and converting them into better uses and more conforming to the spirit of our vocation, that is, by offering rich donations to the Church or by instituting perpetual foundations or by improving the property of the commanderies, which are the fund and patrimony of the Religion. And Reginaldo *lib. 30 tract. 3. n. 98* speaking in general of the beneficiaries of Military Orders (also when Ecclesiastical Beneficiaries are their commanderies) says that in virtue of the vow of poverty, that which improves the revenue of the benefice or commandery must not be assigned to the poor, according to the ecclesiastical precept but reserve it to their Order, to which the Pope assigned such revenue and in such manner has put it to pious use, because military Religions being instituted for the common benefit of Christendom, all property given to them is meant as used in pious deeds. The proper maintenance of our Brethren does not exclude donations to other Brethren, even of large amounts to be applied for the service of the Religion, that is, for the employment of Captain of the Galley or of Ambassador or other similar, because in such case the Religious does not transfer that sum but applies it in actual benefit of the Religion; and although many authors question whether a Religious may give a considerable sum to another of the same Religion without just cause whatsoever, in our Religion however it is sure that one cannot by virtue of a decision of the Veneranda Camera, confirmed by the Ven. Council, which condemned a Brother to give back to the Spoil (spoglio) of another Brother a large sum, which during his lifetime (sua vita durante) he had donated to him, as being excessive and without any title, other than mere liberality *Audienz. Camer. 7. Septembris 1620. Cons. 20. Maggio 1622"*.

"The proper maintenance of our Brethren admits donations by way of compensation. Indeed, since this is necessary for the good administration of temporal property, also because remunerative donation is rather the payment of a debt than a gift, according to the common teaching of the Doctors. Moreover remuneration can be made with the advantage of the benefit received *D. Thom. 2.2. quaest. 106. art. 6.* Also exceeding one third, as if evaluating the benefit at 300 *scudi* donating 400 for it. *Sanch. Matrim lib. 6. disput. 6. n. 9. Navar. de reddit. quaest. 1. n. 91".*

"The proper maintenance of our Brethren does not forbid making moderate donations solely by title of liberality. Because if they can also make donations, provided the amount be moderate, not only the beneficiaries Sanch. *consig. lib. 2, cap. 2. dub. 4. n. 2. Molin. de justit. disput. 145.* but also the Religious to whom is granted the permission to spend in honest use; and some say in particular one can moderately make donations to parents, who are already rich, for reason of gratitude due to parentage. Sanch *moral. lib. 7. cap. 19 num. 98 & 104.*; the same rules may be applied to the Religious of St. John, even with some greater liberality, like those leading a secular life and professing a noble and military life: norms which tolerate even demand liberality, a virtue very suitable to the status of noble persons for their civil life".

Chapter VIII

Legislation analogous to the above Principles

On the guidance of these principles *Stat. XVII of this title* laid down the prohibition to our Religious from transferring immovable property acquired by them, and at the same time they were granted the full enjoyment of life annuity of their intakes. By *Ordinaz. 8 of this title* the last Sacred Chapter General of 1776 vested the Sacred Complete Council (Sagro Consiglio Compito) with authority of granting the faculty of disposing of the abovementioned acquests, when prior to the cited Statute such authority was reserved to the Sacred Chapter General.

Regarding the second part of this Statute many moralists of credit, amongst whom Molina and Sanchez, already quoted, and followed by

Lezzana[72] - made a mistake of no minor importance; they have taught that our Religious can give and dispose liberally of their savings accruing from revenues of the commanderies, also setting up elder brother's inheritance and primogeniture, alleging throughout that the superiors of our Sacred Order allow it - which is not true; therefore the Sagra Ruota Romana in *Lithuana Donationis inserita dopo il voto 249. del Constantini al n. 25.* proscribed as erroneous such opinion.

To the same Sacred Complete Council (Sagro Consiglio Compito) is reserved the authority to grant the faculty of disposing of immovable property acquired in these islands of Malta and Gozo in virtue of *Stat. XVIII of this title*: in this law there is the proviso that having obtained this permission at the time of the last illness it remains ineffective and as such the disposition is of no validity.

From the contents of the two cited Statutes it results that for immovable property outside these islands, the permission granted by the Sacred Complete Council to the Religious during his last illness is valid. In truth the motive of this diversity is not understood, since the immovable property of these islands is of the same nature of the immovable situated in other regions.

To the Grandmaster is prohibited by *Stat X della Regola* the transfer of prerogatives, preeminences and revenues of the magistracy (Magisterio); only the Chapter General has the power of granting him permission. Truly this supreme Tribunal is entrusted by the cited law to regulate its decree in view of legitimate causes.

---

[72] *QQ regul. part. 2. cap. 5. n. 29.*

Chapter IX

Other Sanctions relating to the Vow of Poverty

By Ordinaz 9 della Regola to Commandeurs is permitted the free sale of immovables acquired by them for payment of rents not satisfied by their tenants or occupiers; as is also expressed by Ordinaz. cited as *per amministrazione dovutagli*. One cannot deny that the expression is very laconic and therefore obscure. The meaning seems to be that if the administrator of the Commandery in the liquidation of accounts is debtor to the Commandeur, and in settlement he has acquired an immovable of the debtor, he can freely transfer that immovable, but the cited law requires that the acquest in the said manner is evident by sentence given by a judge. For this reason if the acquest were evident by public instrument, by which the debtor, after having acknowledged his debt, had given in payment one or more immovables, the Commandeur cannot sell it; this legitimate consequence conforms to the contents of the cited Ordinance.

Here the doubt arises: whether a Religious, owner of immovables, which do not pertain to the Religion but have been acquired by him, and he also finds himself adjudicated for payment of rents or for residue of administration on immovable of the debtor, is included in the privilege of the cited Ordinance? The law makes reference only to Commandeurs. The subject does not admit interpretations wider than the terms mean, by which the law is conceived. In the circumstance this reflection soon presents itself: if it gives the faculty of transferring property acquired with revenue of the same immovables of the Religion, with what greater reason one must presume, that it is also meant to be applicable for acquest made from revenue of property, which is not directly of the Religion, but acquired by the Religion through its Religious? But we have the convincing answer: it were proper that it be conceded, but in effect it was not conceded. The omitted case remains at the disposition of the common law, which is, that the Religious cannot dispose of each of his acquests.

One observes here that of the immovables acquired in the said manner, the cited *Ordinaz. 9.* allows sale only during lifetime and no other disposition, remembering that the Commandeur must obtain money for his own use; the circumstance wanted to have an immovable in payment. It was quite just to allow him to sell in order to have money. But if he retains the immovable, abandoning the idea of selling it, then it is understood that he has bought the immovable with the money accruing from his credit; this in consequence is one of those acquests, of which it is prohibited by our statutes to dispose during lifetime and after death.

Our Religious still have the free authority of disposing of a house acquired in the city of Valletta, Vittoriosa, Senglea, Cospicua and in the suburb of Vilhena [Floriana] granted to them by *Ordinaz 10 of this title*, provided however they do not owe the Treasury one hundred *scudi* on the day of sale if it is irrevocable, but if it is revocable on the day of demise.

On the subject the Sagra Ruota Romana in *Melevitana Domus 29. Marzo 1722 avanit Corio* confirmed by *Falconieri Decis. 6. sotto il titolo de donation* stipulated that if the Religious, who disposed irrevocably of the house, died debtor to the Treasury, it should be reimbursed by the donee.

Here doubt arises: a Religious acquires in the said four cities or Borgo two, three or more adjacent houses and those either with new construction or otherwise converts them into one, whether he can dispose of all thus combined together or of one in terms of the Ordinance. I answer that if of the two or three adjacent houses together with the new construction he formed one house, to me it seems that this would be the case contemplated by the Ordinance, because it contains the faculty of one house either acquired or constructed as would be in the preceding case; but if of the three houses after the purchase or other acquest the same structure is retained and only connected together, then I believe the disposition allows only one of the three [houses].

Chapter X

The Vow of Poverty in respect of Patrimonial Property

To dispose of patrimonial immovables the Grandmaster has the authority to grant permission to our Religious as *per Stat. XVI of this title*.

By patrimonial immovables the cited statute defines all immovable property devolving to the Religious through inheritance, succession, legacy and other disposition of his ancestors and relatives.

Ordinance 3 of this title does not include in this magistral permission immovables purchased by the Religious with money derived from patrimonial property, because they did not come to him by inheritance, succession or legacy of his relatives.

Ordinance 4 della Regola contemplates immovables purchased with money obtained from the sale of patrimonial property; these should be considered new acquests by the Religious and hence they are not included in the mentioned magistral permission.

The same law limits this rule in case the sale has been made to effect the new acquest; one mentions this because it is desired that the Religious requests and obtains from the Grandmaster the faculty to sell in order to purchase subsequently, and that within the term of two years he must justify he has purchased with the money obtained from the sale of patrimonial property.

Here doubt arises whether this Ordinance comprises exchanges of immovable property with immovable property. I believe yes, because according to the rule of Common law (Diritto Comune) in *Legge fin. ff. de rer. Permut* and in *cap. Nulli de Reb. non alien.* exchange is defined as purchase and the Religious changes title of his ownership; and it is no more through succession, inheritance or legacy of his relatives, but in virtue of exchange; consequently that Religious, who intends to enter into such contract, would do well to premise the formality indicated in the cited Ordinance.

Some lawyers argue, whether in virtue of the permission granted by the Grandmaster to dispose of patrimonial property, the Religious, who has obtained such permission can revoke the will (testament) made before his profession, Card. Petra[73] maintains for several reasons and with authority that that faculty does not absolutely arrive to this point. Today however the contrary opinion is accepted having been considered as the most correct in view of the decisions delivered by the Sagra Ruota Romana entitled *Melevitana Immissionis inserite dopo il voto 249 del Costantini*.

Stat. XIV of this title prohibits our Religious from making a Will, instituting heirs and donations *causa mortis*; by permission given by the Grandmaster it is allowed to dispose of a quint of their money, movables, gold- and silverwares, credits and self-moving items.

This statute reads: "We ordain that the permission to dispose be invalid and insufficient to those who when disposing will be liquid debtors to our Treasury (Comun Tesoro) in the amount which exceeds hundred *scudi* in currency of Malta" explained by Caravita.[74] Provided at the time of the disposition they are no liquid debtors of the Treasury etc. Therefore, if the person who makes the disposition on the day he was disposing was not a debtor, but he was so on the day of his demise, the disposition is valid.

---

[73] *Ad Constit. Apost. Const. 5. Bened. XII, n. 17.*
[74] *Nel Compend. tit. 5. Para. Disporre.*

Chapter XI

Simulated Contracts

It is prohibited to our Religious to enter into simulated contracts as per *Stat. XXI of this title* under pain of infamy, of privation of the commanderies to Commandeurs and to other Religious of seniority culminating in *Stat. XXII susseguente.*

Any obligation by the Religious is considered simulated whereby is convenanted the fulfilment after the demise of the Religious by *Ordinaz 11 of this title.*

The second part of the cited *Stat XXI of this title* merits to be commented upon with some attention. Religious are prohibited from making promissory notes, obligations, donations, stipends or debts. Then it is prescribed that if during his lifetime the Religious had not provided for after demise the fulfilment of such obligations in favour of whom they had been made, they are to be considered simulated and made as fraud for the Religion and therefore not extinguishable.

This law in respect of policies of debts and obligations by Brethren not provided with commanderies is useless in view of the setting up of the Tribunal known as of the debtors by Chapter General of 1777 by *Ordinaz. 13 of this title* and the subsequent provident disposition of *Ordinaz. 14,* which condemns as null and of no validity any obligation, public or private, made by Brethren without the necessary permission or decree of the said Tribunal with the consequence that the creditor cannot claim anything, neither during lifetime nor after death.

Therefore said second part of the abovementioned statute remains applicable to debtor Commandeurs, Bailiffs and Priors. It is true that they are prohibited from making these written obligations, but once having made such obligations they may be compelled to satisfy them during their lifetime, since the Statute requires that they be considered simulated and false if during lifetime the creditor did not procure that they be satisfied.

One understands that the creditor has procured the fulfilment of the promise if he brought the debtor to court, and if he obtained from the competent Tribunals the executive letters, or has practised such and many diligences as to persuade, that the obligation was not simulated, neither made to elude the Religion in the spoil (spoglio) of the Commandeur or Bailiff bound by the obligation.

However it is true that our Sacred Order is very humane in the execution of the cited *Statute XXI* and especially with the families of the Religious. *Costantini nel voto 249* gives us an example. A Commandeur of ours administrator of the patrimony of his nieces confessed in one of his books of being a debtor to them for a considerable sum. The Religion supported by the cited Statute and by Common Law (Dritto Comune) could have in all fairness refused the payment; having however considered that the Religious had in fact administered the patrimony of the nieces; that he was most correct, that before he died he had ratified his debt with the confessor and that he had not disposed, though he was empowered, of his patrimonial immovables, the Sacred Order agreed to a most advantageous transaction with the nieces of the Commandeur.

The written obligations of debt by the Brethren residing in the Convent, if they are supported by the signature and seal of the Marshal, are valid at all times as per *Ordinaz. 12 of this title*; exactly as if they had been authenticated by decree of the Tribunal of Debtors (Tribunale dei Debitori). This is declared by *Ordinaz. 19 of the present title*.

Chapter XII

Spoils *(Dispropriamento)*

Every Religious is burthened by *Statute XXIII della Regola* of making every year his spoil, that is to say, the description of all that he has, also of all the credits and debts. Residents in the Convent have to seal and submit them either to the Grandmaster or to the Procurators of the Treasury. Those residing outside the Convent must submit them, also in sealed form, to the Provincial Chapter in order to be kept in a box, which is deposited there for this purpose.

The infirm Brethren outside the Convent must call two Brethren residing in the nearest places, one of whom is a chaplain, if possible, and manifest all their assets, by drawing up in writing a minute description of every item. This writing must be supported with the seal of the infirm Brother, and of the two Brethren compiling the description. It must then be delivered to whom in that country or province administers the interests of the Treasury, that is, either to the Receiver (Ricevidore) or to the Procurator of the Treasury *Statuto XXIV of this title.* The infirm Brother who contravenes this law is punished, if he recovers from his illness, by penalties inflicted by our laws against the disobedient.

The Brethren who assisted in the compilation of the spoil are bound by secrecy in terms of the cited Statute under pain of privation of the commandery for ten years in the case of commandeurs for the non-observance of secrecy whilst the infirm Brother is still alive; if they are ordinary Religious the Statute states as follows: *where legal action is taken it is proceeded with according to the justice of the Religion.* It appears that they must be punished with arbitrary penalty, because this is what is meant: *according to the justice of the Religion.*

Chapter XIII

Conclusions

A Knight having debts before the regular profession renounces all his present estate in favour of his relatives. After his regular profession he receives an inheritance, which then upon his death devolves on the Religion. It is questioned as to whom pertains the obligation to pay the said debts? The Sagra Ruota Romana[75] decided that settlement rests with the renouncers.

The motives were that in the act of profession because of the preceding renunciation *ex illius persona nihil ad Religionem pervenisse, sicque, neque illam ad Equitis debita teneri, cum ille sine bonis Religionem fuerit ingressus, nec illi in aliquo Religio successerat:* the inheritance accruing on the deceased, being according to the general opinion of moralists, an acquest directly of the Religion, was not subject to debt, as if it does not concern the debtor.

The good Religious must always hold in the greatest consideration the article concerning game.

Theologians define game as a contract whereby the players put in peril their own property in the hope of acquiring that of others[76].

Game of its very nature is no vice, when it has as its aim licit amusement, which St. Thomas calls *eutrapelia*,[77] because *pertinet ad virtutem.*

Illicit is that game in which fortune prevails over art, like the game of cards and of dies. Moralists agree that the Religious playing cards and dies commits mortal sin; they argue so: in cap. *Inter dilectos de excess. Prelator, etc.* is prescribed the disposition of the cleric who plays cards.

---

[75] Dec. 233, part. 2 Recent.
[76] *Lezzana tom 2, verb. ludus quoad Reg. n. 2.*
[77] *22. qu. 16. art. 2.*

The most heavy penalty of the deposition is not inflicted by Canon Law (Dritto Canonico) but for mortal sin. The inference which results therefrom is the said proposition.

However it is limited by the same Moralists, whenever this type of game is for mere and simple amusement and for small amounts.

These principles may be applied to our Religious.

Undoubtedly those Knights and Religious who play perversely for considerable sums sin against their vow, because they put in jeopardy their property, of which they are only users since the property belongs to the Sacred Order in virtue of the Vow of Poverty and this is the common opinion by Theologians[78] *Ludentes tamen Religiosi notabilem summam pecuniae, vel alterius rei pretio estimabilis peccant contra votum Paupertatis.*

There are authors, among them Diana[79] who conclude that it is licit to our Religious to gamble all that property of which they can dispose either in virtue of the faculties conceded by the Grandmaster empowered by the Statutes to grant such faculties or by the Statutes themselves, that is, to say, they can gamble the price of a house purchased in the four cities of this island and in the Borgo Vilhena [Floriana], the price of patrimonial immovables, of which they obtained the permission to dispose, the price of immovables purchased in this island of Malta and Gozo after having obtained from the Sacred Council the permission to dispose. Lezzana however[80] basing on the authority of accredited moralists indicates this opinion as being erroneous and it seems, that he is correct: *"licit autem aliqui putent Religiosum obtinentem generalem licentiam a sua Superiore donandi, aut expendendialiquam quantitatem posse eam ludo exponere etc. verumtamen tenendum est contrarium, nisi horum Theologorum placitum intelligatur de parva, & moderate quantitate, & de ludo alias honesto, nec*

---

[78] *Lezzana verbo Ludus, quoad Regul n. 10.*
[79] *Part. 3, tract. 2 dub. 98.*
[80] *Verb. Ludus quoad Regul. n. 12.*

prohibito ipsi Religioso; eo quod licentia illa non extendatur, nec extendi possit nisi ad usus licitos, & honestos". Truly it is impossible to accept that our legislators in giving to our Religious the power to transfer patrimonial immovables, the houses in this city and the immovables in these islands with such laxity of the Vow of Poverty have wanted to grant such power in order to use it for game, when *Ordinances 12, 13 delle Probiz. e Pene* prohibit every kind of game both of surplus, as they are called, and of commerce every time there is excessive sum for which one may play.

Whether our Religious can constitute with considerable capitals annuity rents was discussed on other occasions. The system of the Religion was always to consider this type of contracts totally contrary to the Vow of Poverty. I know, it was that some of our Religious intended to enter into contracts of such rents with the Common Treasury itself and were excluded. The Sagra Ruota Romana however allowed them according to several decisions it has delivered[81] Caravita gives this advice: "The annuity rent can be constituted by our Brethren either because of the need to maintain themselves decently in their status, by which they improve their revenues, as is usual in the purchase of this rent or if notable advantage is derived not only to the Religious but also to the Religion".

---

[81] *Dopo Palma dec. 107*

Book Three

Chapter I

Elections

Having spoken in Book One of the Conventual Bailiffs, Priors and Capitular Bailiffs, it is considered appropriate to explain in this third book the legislation relating to the manner in which they are elected and all that there is contained in title 13 of our Code.

The general rule prescribed by *Stat. III dell'Elez.* is that to the Grandmaster and Ordinary Council (Consiglio Ordinario) pertains exclusively from any other Tribunal the power to elect Bailiffs and Priors with the intended expression of the cited Statuto: *saving however always the nomination of the Langue.*

The interpretative observance of this last sanction produced in the vacancies of the mentioned dignities the routine, that when the vacancy occurs, either through demise or through resignation or privation, the respective Langue is convened and the vacated dignity is restored in favour of who has requested it. Then the candidate presents himself before the Ordinary Council producing the justificative extract of the deliberation of the Langue of the nomination obtained with the declaration by the Secretary to the Treasury that he is not a debtor to the Treasury requesting either the candidate himself or through an attorney of his to be appointed.

Chapter II

Remarks on Statute IV of the Election

To the cited Statute there follows the fourth, which merits the most accurate consideration. It begins: "We ordain that every time that the Master and Ordinary Council shall proceed with the election of a Conventual Bailiff, after having heard those who usually request the Bailiwick, having first examined the conduct and the merits of those, who make the request by those sitting in the Council, without reserving order but according to what they decided before, ballot is carried out, the Master receives the solemn oath taken on the Cross of the habit of the Bailiffs and Priors who will be present in the Council for making the election, that they will elect as Bailiff a person suitable, useful, worthy and of major merits, taking into consideration rather his ability and merits than the seniority".

The formality in such election as that of Conventual Bailiffs of giving the prescribed oath is today not practised any more. But as to preferring merit to seniority in all occasions was determined by decisions of the Sagra Ruota Romana especially in Melvitana *Dignitarum*[82] where one reads the following highly good consideration: *summoque jure in dignitatibus Conventualibus semper a Nostro Sacro Auditorio servata fuit praelatio a Statutis concessa Equiti majoris benemerentiae supra Equitem antianum hanc benemerentiam non habentem: cum enim Equites natimac ad hujusmodi Dignitates promoventur, evadant capita Lingitarum suarumque nationum, nec non etiam Consiliarii Magni-Magistri, & dicantur columnae Religionis, dum illam gubernant, & regunt sub ejusdem Magni-Magistri auctoritate etc. Hinc simplex antiatitas, quae de per se nullam dat aptitudinem, & benemerentian pro Gubernio, & REGIMINE RELIGIONIS, PRAELATIONEM tribuere - nequit in ossequen. dict. dignitatibus.*

---

[82] *12 Giugno 1733 avanti Rezzonico, poi Clemente XIII, §, 7.*

In theory it admirable because it is most useful for the service of the Sacred Order; but most difficult it is in my opinion weighing the merits of the candidates.

By merit one understands ordinarily in the Republics the spontaneous service for the country and the will always ready to render such service, being employed without the least view of interest in such manner that every operation made in the execution of the laws is called fulfilment of the proper duty and not merit.

This merit was explained by the Sagra Ruota in the quoted decision, which meant to prescribe Statute III *dell'Elezioni: Benemerentia quippe, de qua loquitur Statutum, intelligenda est illa non pro operibus praestitis ad mensuram propriae obligationis, sed pro iis, qua sunt extra debitum.*

There is another principle as regards our Sacred Order, that all the posts in and outside the Convent are appointed to a great extent by the Grandmaster and some few by the Conventual Bailiffs with the successive confirmation of the Council either Ordinary or Complete (Compito).

With the guidance of these principles one can take the liberty of examining the posts, which the Sagra Ruota Romana in the quoted decision and in the other entitled *Melevitana Dignitatis Magnae Commendae*,[83] considered productive of merit or not.

In the first *Dignitatum* it did not consider worthy of merit of the candidate for having performed the four caravans, renewed the *Cabrei* (Land Registers) and carried out improvements in the commanderies entrusted to him, for the very good reason that "*Ea quae fiunt, & fieri debent ab omnibus vigore praecedentis obligationis non inducunt illam benemerentiam, de qua mentionem fecit Statutum in conferendis Dignitatibus Conventualibus.* "

---

[83] *Dec. 13, dopo il voto 200, di Costantini.*

The posts of the Commendatore dei Forni (of the bakeries), Prud Homme delle opere (Comptroller), Procurator of the respective Langue, Lieutenant of the Grand Treasurer and of the Hospitaller were not considered of merit in view of *che hujusmodi officia, vel tamquam lucrosa, & tenuis incumbentiae, & laboris; vel tamquam comperata ex debito justitiae ratione antianitatis nullum praestare possunt argumentum specialis benemerentiae.*

On the contrary as proof of merit in the said decision was appreciated the biennial role of Castellan though lucrative and not incurring much labour. The office of Commendator of the Sacred Infirmary, though strenuous but of not indifferent profit.

In the other decision cited above *Meleviatana Dignitatis Magnae-Commendae* were declared worthy of merit those who for more than ten years have resided in the Convent, because the residence of ten years in the Convent is the fulfilment of a duty stipulated by *Statute XI dell' Elez.* in order to receive the Conventual Dignities, whence it is of merit to have resided there even for more years; likewise who for two years had commanded any one of the galleys of this Sacred Order; who performed the duties of Prud Homme of the major Conventual church; who was Receiver of the Sacred Order outside the Convent; who equally for the whole two years was Padrone (Master) of galley. It was argued in the cited decision, whether this post gave merit; it was decided that if one performed such activity voluntarily and not in fulfilment of the duty of the caravans, it had to be considered absolutely worthy of merit.

These conclusions are in truth pleasing and good, but a judge must think with much sobriety in this type of disputes. It is good to remember that the nominations for the posts are dependent on the selection by the superiors and not on the decision of the Religious; if he has the misfortune of being forgotten when vacancies occur, so it is not his fault in the miserable necessity of seeing the Conventual dignities taken over by the fiernaldi [his juniors].

The dignity of Captain General of the Galleys and of Captain of the other galleys is considered as most worthy of merit. Well, but these posts entail a considerable expense, properly assigned to the rich; who is not rich must be sure that competing with one who was General or Captain must have the humiliation of being deferred.

It appears from these my remarks that the statute is useless; I am not saying this, but I believe that the only merit of residence in the Convent is the all important factor, because who is here present shows the positive desire of serving the Sacred Order; in consequence if he does not in fact serve the Order it must be the fault of the government, which has not assigned him any duties.

In the second part of the cited *Statute IV* there is this other disposition: "And in such manner we ordain that they be similarly elected and created the Prior of the church, and the other Priors and Capitular Bailiffs".

In respect of the Prior of the major church is observed exactly this disposition; seniority of the candidates is absolutely not taken into consideration but the quality of merits determines the selection; of the other Priors however and Capitular Bailiffs we have several decisions of the Sagra Ruota Romana, by which it assures us that a constant ancient custom derogated the transcribed second part of the cited statute by stipulating that for the Capitular dignities only seniority is taken into considered *nec officit Stat. V. de Elect.* in the old Codex, and 4 in the new Codex: *nam illud locum obtinet in dictis Dignitatibus Conventualibus, secus autem in ceteris extra Conventum, in quibus usu receptum non fuit, nec aliter a sanct. Mem. Paulo V. illud fuit confirmatum quam conditione adjecta si est in usu: quod autem dictum Statutum in ceteris Dignitatibus extra Conventum usu receptum non sit liquido constat ex Decisionibus coram Dunquet. 166, n. 7, coram Coccin. 1169, n. 11, cor. Crispo decis. 475, n. 3, tom 3.* [84]

---

[84] *Melevitanae Bajulivatus S. Stephani 6 Maggio 1735, § 17, avanti Calcagnini.*

The statute winds up: "always observed the reinstatement of the Langues according to ancient custom". If by the word *osservata* (observed) is to be meant the necessity of conforming to the deliberation of the Langue, then it would not be that free election, which the statute prescribes; thence that *osservata* etc. the Sagra Ruota Romana explained in the quoted *Melevitana Dignitarum*, that before resorting to election in the Sacred Council the request must be submitted to the respective Langue and obtained the reinstatement which characterises one simple nomination *quae sit a Lingua Emo Magno Magistro, ejusque Ven. Consilio, quibus competit Jus conferendi.*

Chapter III

Requisites for the reception of Conventual and Capitular Bailiwicks

The first requisite for being elected or promoted to the dignities both Conventual and Capitular is that of having been received in the rank of Knight of Justice, that is to say, having made the proofs of Nobility and Legitimacy, according to the laws of the respective Langue or Priorate[85] in a manner that for the same dignities are ineligible the knights commonly known as of Grace.[86]

Statute IX of this title excludes from the reception of the said dignities those absent from the Convent at the time that action is being taken for the filling of the vacancy or by selection considering best that "the residence in the Convent of the senior Brethren is very essential for many reasons and particularly for rendering the services which are necessary for the administration."

The same law however wanted to have them considered as being present in the Convent those entrusted with a post or office of the Religion

---

[85] *Stat. V dell Elez.*
[86] *Stat. V di ques. titolo.*

outside the Convent. And likewise are considered excepted those who are hindered legitimately from being in the Convent.

But in order that the impediment may be considered legitimate, it is prescribed that as soon as the impediment occurs it must be signified to the Grandmaster and Council with the justificative document of same or of the Provincial Assembly or of the Chapter or of the respective Prior. Nevertheless according to two decisions of the Sagra Ruota Romana whatsoever justification different from that indicated in the Statute absolutely does not help however legal it may be: *"At in casu assertae infirmitatis Equitis de Niozelles justificata neutiquam fuit ex publica, & authentica attestatione, vel Capituli Provincialis, vel Prioris, vel Assembleae, multoque minus statimhaec. Et primo quoque tempore trasmisso fuit ad Magnum Magistrum, & Venerandum Concilium, idcirco admitti non potest probatio haec illegitima, quaeque nulla in parte cumulata dignoscitur ad tramites legis, pro evitandis fraudibus certam femant praescribentis etc.*[87] "

The third requisite is the seniority of fifteen years. The Statute[88] is worded in terms as to give rise to doubt regarding the time from which this seniority should commence to be counted, whether from the day of the reception or from the day of the profession. It is worded as follows: "Therefore we ordain that none of our Brethren may be accepted or elected Bailiff or Prior who has not carried our Habit fifteen years to be reckoned from the day on which he first came in the Convent and was received and that under true obedience of our Order has lived without incurring any blame".

If one considers the purpose of the Statute, it appears that this seniority for Bailiwicks and Priorates must be reckoned from the day of profession. The purpose is expressed in the statute itself: "It is to them convenient and necessary, that those who have to be entrusted with the

---

[87] *Decis. 13, e 14 dopo il voto 200, di Costantini.*
[88] *Stat. X dell'Elez.*

government and state of the Order be versed in that and have experience of our affairs and this cannot be done unless they have practised in it for a long time:"

Such practice and experience in the affairs of the Sacred Order is acquired by the exercise of posts. These can be conferred only to the professed and not to novices. Consequently at the moment of their profession they cannot have that experience, which the legislator desires in the persons destined for the government.

In the second place the terms are most significant: *that has not carried our Habit for fifteen years*. Our Habit is the White Cross that one carries after one's profession; and *who has lived under the true obedience of our Order*: true obedience is that which one swears with the solemn Vow.

But otherwise the constant interpretative observance of this statute never disputed is that seniority, a requisite for the dignities, was always calculated from the day of reception.

The fourth requisite is the ten-year residence in the Convent either continuous or with intervals[89] which years of Conventual residence apply as a general rule to all the employed outside the Convent in the service of the Sacred Religion, as are the Receivers (Ricevidori), who benefit of yet six months, a term prescribed to them to present themselves in the Convent with their accounts[90], to the Procurators of the Treasury outside the Convent[91], to the Brethren who arm by permission of the Council or are taken by the infidels being in the service of the Religion[92] or in coming to the Convent[93].

---

[89] *Stat. XII delle Commende.*
[90] *Stat. XII Commend, Stat. LXX del Tesoro.*
[91] *Stat. LXX Tesoro.*
[92] *Ord. 23 dell' Ufficio dei Fratelli.*
[93] *Stat. XIV delle Commende.*

The fifth requisite of having well administered the commanderies, with which the candidate may be provided by any title, including also the *Camere Magistrali* by means of the processes known to us of the Visitation of improvements and of having renewed the *Cabrei* (Land Registers). Here however it is proper to note that this requisite must compete with regard to the processes of improvements, if the pretending Conventual or Capitular Bailiwick is found to have enjoyed for five continuous years the Commanderies of Justice, six the Commanderies of Grace and seven the *Camere Magistrali* (Magistral Chambers) according to what is declared by *Stat. XXXVI of the Commanderies.*

The same rule applied to the *Cabrei* before the last Sacred Chapter General. The absent Commandeur in the renewal of the *Cabrei* was not punishable with the incapacity of being promoted to the dignities, if not after the five, six and seven years of enjoyment aboveindicated. But today that we have the new sanction (however for the Langues of Italy, of Aragon, of Germany, Anglo-Bavarian and Castile)[94] that on the expiration of the twenty-five years stipulated by the Statute the holder must commence in the twenty-sixth year the Cabreo, in the twenty-seventh continue it, and in the twenty-eighth complete it; and this without regard, whether he enjoyed the commanderies in the mentioned years. Consequently it becomes a requisite to whom is found in case of having satisfied the said obligations.

If having resided five years in the Commandery either of Justice or of Grace be a requisite to be elected Bailiff and consequently an exception, not having done so, to be excluded, the resolution is doubtful. The Sagra Ruota Romana frankly decided *Residentia qinqennalis in Commenda, ut cumque necessaria pro assecutione alterius Commendae, non autem requiritur ad effectum, ut quis promoveri & elegi possit ad Dignitates Conventuales, quae non titulo Melioramenti optantur, sed per electionem conferuntur, habita ratione majoris idoneitatis, & benemerentiae.*

---

[94] *Ord. 44 delle Comm.*

It does not appear nevertheless that the Statute[95] which prescribes the requisite of the five-year residence applies to the options of the Commanderies. Whilst it clearly prescribes: "that the Brethren who will have been once provided with any Commandery, cannot benefit from another, before they have personally resided in the Commandery for five years".

Chapter IV

Ambassadors

Statute XIV of this title prescribes to the Grandmaster and Ordinary Council the appointment of an ordinary ambassador to the Holy See for a term of three years with the decision however to confirm him so *many times as they will consider opportune.*

To the same Tribunal is entrusted the election of the Extraordinary Ambassadors by *Ordinaz. 6 of the same title* with this singularity, that the deputation, in order to be considered ordained, there must be two thirds of the votes; but then for the election of the Ambassador suffices the plurality.

Chapter V

Captains General of Land and of Sea

The Captain General of the Land Force, that is, of the land troops is elected by the Grandmaster and by the Sacred Complete Council with three fourths of the votes; he must be of the Ven. Langue of Auvergne, if in that Langue is found a person suitable for that command; in case to the contrary a person from another Langue is chosen for that occasion

---

[95] *Stat. XLII delle Comm.*

with the expressed declaration that it is not intended to prejudice the right of the said Langue.

The Captain General of the naval force must be of the Ven. Langue of Italy, if there is a suitable person; otherwise from another Langue is chosen under the same condition without prejudice of the said Langue, owner of this dignity[96].

Chapter VI

The Castellan

The Grandmaster together with the Complete Council elects every two years the Castellan. This post goes the run to all the Ven. Langues by turn, a professed knight from each Langue for a term of two years and who has at least eight years residence in the Convent. The custom is that the Pilier of the Langue, from which the knight is to be elected, submits the list of the professed knights who have the requisite of the described seniority. This is read out in the Complete Council; then the Grandmaster nominates one of them and voting is proceeded with.

The newly elected then takes the oath in the hands of the Grandmaster of distributing Justice.

In case the Castellan dies or renounces, in the course of the two-year term then another knight from the same Langue[97] is elected by the said Complete Council.

All the duties of the Castellan are the following as recorded in the new Codice Municipale (Municipal Code).

The Castellan, following his election, and having made the oath in terms of the statutes of our Order XVII and XVIII title of the elections, and hav-

---

[96] *Stat. XV dell' Elez.*
[97] *Cons. 20, Luglio 1638, e 5 Xbre 1644.*

ing taken possession from the Ven. Bailiff Seneschal commences the exercise of his ministry.

His precise duty is to supervise that justice is administered to one and all with promptness and correctness.

He will assist in the compilation of criminal proceedings, especially in serious lawsuits and must intervene in all the reports which are made to us by the Tribunal of the Gran Corte (Grand Court) of the Castellania.

He will intervene with the Judge at the hearings which will be held on the appointed days.

He will assist in all the visits which the Gran Corte of the Castellania makes to the public notaries of the four cities of Valletta, Vittoriosa, Senglea and Cospicua in the public archives, to the Deputy of the Public Registry and to all the others which the Criminal Judge and the Fiscal Advocate [Attorney General] of the said Gran Corte will carry out.

He can only order the imprisonment of criminals caught red-handed or when there is danger of their escaping or asylum or in case of trifle matters which merit only correction to have them remitted in the prisons of the Gran Corte of the Castellania.

In all other instances without the approval of the Judge he will not be permitted to order the imprisonment of accused; neither will it be in his decision indistinctively to release from prison, enlarge or restrict the prisons without decree by the Judge.

He will not be permitted to speak to imprisoned criminials in the secret prisons without the intervention of the Judge and Advocate or Fiscal Procurator; neither will he be able to accord permission to the Advocates or to others to speak to them without the said intervention.

Said ministers, jailer and assistant jailer in case of contravention to what is prescribed in the preceding paragraphs 6, 7 and 8 are bound to report to us under pain of losing their office, post and others as we deem fit.

He shall not allow the carrying out of any condemnation with corporal punishment without our previous knowledge.

He will receive on the first day of September the oath of the officials appointed *pro Tribunali sedenti* (for the presiding Tribunals) in the civil hall of the Gran Corte of the Castellania together with the Judges and Fiscal Advocate.

The Castellan will receive the oath in the form prescribed in the new compilation, of all the Advocates who will have been issued by us with the licence to patronize the lawsuits in the Tribunals.

He is bound to ensure the carrying out of the commendations and sentences delivered in matters adjudicated and the two conforming sentences proffered by the Gran Corte of the Castellania and by the supreme Magistrate of Justice, availing himself of the approval of the Judge of the Gran Corte of the Castellania, whenever one operates in execution of commendations or of sentences of the same Gran Corte delivered in matters adjudicated; or of that Judge who will have less charge, or of the *Consigliere Commissario*, who will be appointed by the President of the said supreme Magistrate, likewise the decrees of the same supreme Magistrate, whenever they have to be carried out with the approval of the appointed *Consigliere Commissario*.

And if the two conforming sentences will have been proffered, one by the Gran Corte Capitaniale, and the other by the Magistrate of the city of Notabile [Mdina], their execution must be made by the Judge or by the Jurats [Aldermen] of the said Tribunals, who will have less charge.

But if said two conforming sentences will be proffered one either by the abovesaid Capitaniale or by the above said Magistrate of the city of Notabile, and the other by the Supreme Magistrate of Justice, the execution of the proffered sentences is encumbent on one of the said Magistrates, who will have less charge, and being incumbent on the supreme Magistrate of Justice, the President will appoint the *Consigliere Commissario* concerned for the execution of the conforming sentences.

At the end of the races, which are held in this city of Valletta on the feasts of St. John the Baptist and St. Roque or others, which we may ordain, together with the Jurats [Aldermen] of the *Universitas* [Commune] of the city of Valletta, he will cause to be distributed the prizes or *pali* to whom they are due. And in case of dispute, it is decided together with the same Jurats without the formality of proceedings, and will ensure that the sentence is carried out, if the succumbing party does not verbally feel aggrieved; otherwise the execution is suspended till our *Cavalerizzo Maggiore* (Master Equerry), superior judge in such matters, has pronounced himself, whose word has to be carried out, remote is the appeal or whatsoever other legal remedy.

It will be his duty to supervise that the *Gran Visconte* [Head of Police], his Lieutenant and Captains make the beat at night and he also will have to go out on the beat in this city of Valletta at the hours which will be detailed to him.

He has to supervise over all the idlers, vagabonds, gamblers, notorious people, and foreigners, carrying out that which is ordained by us; and at the end of each month he will submit a note on these people for further adequate remedy.

He will be bound to give special attention to foreigners, who will be living in this Realm, and will keep a register, in which are entered their name, surname, country of origin, and of the motives of their coming here and of their stay, what they intend doing, and the place earmarked for their stay and residence; and he will cause to observe their behaviour during their domicile; he will also cause to take note of their departure, ship and place, whereto they are leaving and purpose of their journey. He cannot publish without our special permission other *Bandi* (Bans), other than the usual ones in the manner and form expressed in this new compilation.

He will cause to enforce all that which will be ordained by the Jurats of the four cities of Valletta, Vittoriosa, Cospicua and Senglea by under-signing them without being able to alter them, even when they might appear to him to be excessive; the Ven. Bailiff Seneschal is vested as Superior Judge to acknowledge their excessiveness or tenuity, and finding this, to reform and moderate them.

He will cause to ensure the despatch of the patents and bulletins and for these and for the subscriptions of the orders he will charge the usual fees.

He will be bound to attend together with the Judges and the Supreme Magistrate of Justice in all general processions of the major Conventual church of St. John.

In case of his departure, renunciation or death his Lieutenant will be able, without exacting any right whatsoever, to impose new stamps in measures and weights.

Chapter VII

The Lieutenant of the Castellan

The Castellan has his Lieutenant by exclusive appointment by the Grandmaster because of his pre-eminence.

This Lieutenant is usually the Governor of the city of Vittoriosa, called in the Codice Municipale (Municipal Code) *Capitan d'Armi* (Captain of Arms) where there are stipulated the following duties.

The Captain of Arms of the city of Vittoriosa, Knight of our Order, who will be elected by us and will hold the post at our pleasure, will be bound, as Lieutenant of the Castellan, to make the night beat for the said city of Vittoriosa, and for the cities of Cospicua and Senglea; and will supervise that the Captains on night shift make the beat.

He will cause to enforce the observance of our Constitutions regarding the harbour and manderaggio [land-locked creek] and will cause to bring all contraventions and abuses to our knowledge and to the knowledge of our Gran Corte for the opportune remedy.

He will have the power to cause the imprisonment of any criminals caught red-handed and will remit them immediately to the prisons of the Gran Corte of the Castellania.

He cannot exercise jurisdiction of any kind against the person of the criminals, neither commit under any pretext crimes and excesses of any nature, even the most minute, being bound to communicate and remit every incident to the said Gran Corte of the Castellania.

He cannot free from prison any person, even though that person had been imprisoned on his order.

He will have to supervise over idlers, vagabonds, gamblers and other notorious people and besides over foreigners; and will observe the rules relating thereto.

He will grant and give the name to the boats enabling them to stay outside the maderaggio, and to the local and foreign boats the licence to berth.

He will preside over all public functions, which will be held in the parochial church of St. Lawrence in the said city of Vittoriosa, and will take the first seat in the *sedia Giuratale*, which is installed in the said parochial church.

He will take over without any other special authorization or substitution at functions and the office of the Castellan in case of the latter's infirmity or other legitimate impediment.

The Lieutenant of the said Vice Castellan and Captain of Arms holds the same powers, saving those expressed in the Paragraph preceding 33.

In all instances not contained and envisaged in this Compilation he will have to recourse to us in order to receive the opportune orders.

Chapter VIII

The Election of the Grandmaster

The Prior Caravita explains to us so well and with distinction the ceremonial established by Pontiff Urban VIII for the election of the Grandmaster that he left out nothing to others to make further additions. Consequently we have decided that here we reproduce verbatim (*tali quali*) his text.

Pope Urban VIII has changed in many things the old form for electing the Grandmaster, contained in *Stat. 1 lez.* by his Bull, which begins *In specula militantis Ecclesiae* of 3 July 1628 accepted by the Council and registered at the chancery on 23 August of the same year, that we must follow, but according to the ceremonial which His Holiness established by the new Bull of 21 October 1634, by which he declared many things and added others to the first Constitution. The abovementioned *Stat. 1 lez.* remained in force. Only the headings which do not contradict said Bull were retained. The contents of which and of the said Statute reads as follows.

The Grandmaster knowing he is seriously infirm must confide the Bulls, silver dies and secret seal to some good Religious, or command that they be put in safe keeping so that no one may make use of them fraudulently and if he does not do so the Seneschal must soclit him to this *Stat. 1 Elez.*

On the death of the Grandmaster, the Ordinary Council is convened when the said Bulls, dies and seal are broken, and his state funeral with moderation and devotion is announced *Stat. 1, Elez.* deputizing two Knights for the purpose.

This Council although secret is convened with the pealing of bells and nevertheless the Councillors assemble wearing a toga or long robe. The Lieutenant of the deceased Grandmaster presides and there not being a Lieutenant, the most preeminent, until the Lieutenant of the magistracy is elected *Cons. Stat. 28 Nov. 1535.*

Afterwards is convened as early as possible the Council of State or Complete Council. *Ceremonial Cap. 1. Stat. Elez.* although *Stat. 1 Elez.* requires that the obsequies of the Grandmaster being over the Complete Council is convened. The custom is that on the demise of the Grandmaster the Ordinary Council is convened immediately, and afterwards the

Complete Council on that same day, if possible, or at least on the following day, although the Grandmaster has not yet been interred, as was the case on 10 June 1636.

This Council of State decrees matters pertaining to the magistracy.

Which decrees have the force of Chapter General *Stat. 1. Elez.*

Matters pertaining to the magisterium, which are dealt with by the Council of State after the demise of the Grandmaster, are all matters concerning the future election of the Grandmaster, as we shall better explain with the ceremonial in this and in the following chapters, stating that in this Council of State it was customary to make various decrees in favour of the Common Treasury pertaining to the magisterium. But by Apostolic Brief registered in the Chancery on 26. January 1639 ab Incarn. in similar Councils of State neither revenues nor the magistral preeminences could be decreased. For this reason some decrees made in favour of the Treasury and in prejudice to magistral revenues by the Council of State after the demise of Grandmaster Lascaris were soon declared null and void by the Ordinary Council on 18 December 1657.

Sometimes the Council of State has committed to the Ordinary Council to provide for some of the abovementioned matters pertaining to the magisterium by authority of the Chapter General *Cons. di Stat. 16. Sept. 1622.*

At first the Council of State elects the Lieutenant of the magisterium according to the form of the Statutes *Ceremonial Cap. 1.*

Whose office lasts up to the election of the Commendatore of the Election *Stat. 1 Elez.* Each of the Councillors can nominate for Lieutenant whom he wants, and is elected by secret ballot and with the plurality of votes, putting in two urns, one with *ays* and one with *no*. And having been elected he makes the usual oath before the President. But if those nominated are more, then there is a corresponding number of voting-urns, and proceeding with secret ballot, who has the most votes is considered elected, conforming to *Stat. XVIII Cons.* which generally deals with the election to any dignity or office, and stipulates that as many voting-urns as are the proposed candidates, and the election follows with only one scrutiny with the plurality of votes.

The Bishop cannot be elected Lieutenant since he does not administer directly that office; he is not subject (according to some) to correction by the Convent, being released from the Vote of Obedience. But arguing in the Council of State on 14. June 1660, whether the Bishop could be elected Lieutenant, he said he would be satisfied that he is not elected, without prejudice however neither to himself nor to his successors. The Priors of the church can be elected Lieutenants as was Prior Camarasa when the magisterium was vacant on 16 Sept. 1622.

The Lieutenant exercises mere justice and cannot dispense of any Brother Knight or other person, who requests to be admitted to the Habit of Brethren, over any impediment of whatsoever nature or defect, even in virtue of whatsoever privilege or authority; neither can the Council of State and under whatsoever pretext, grant other favours such as conceding the Habit of the Religion et similia. Neither carry out Apostolic Letters directed to the deceased Grandmaster, neither grant favours under penalty of privation of active and passive vote to be incurred *eo ipso*, and the said Lieutenant to be declared excluded by the said Council and nullifying the favour granted by him *Ceremonial Cap. 1.*

Chapter IX

Of the three Deputies for receiving payment from debtors to the Treasury

The Council of State deputizes three faithful and rich Brother Knights from one or from different Langues to receive in the vacant magisterium from debtors of the Treasury in liquid cash all that which they owe and issue to them receipts. They are in duty bound, after the election, to hand over the money to the ministers, to whom it pertains. And payment made otherwise does not satisfy in such manner that they are not considered debtors to the Treasury, to the effect as not to cast their vote *Ceremonial Cap. 2.*

Payment effected by debtors, although the Ceremonial says that it is to be made in cash, however who hands over gold and silver in weight and as effective payment is considered to have fulfilled the obligation; because payment made in such manner frees from debt in virtue of *Ordinaz. 43 Tesoro* notwithstanding that *Stat 11 Tesoro* requires payment in liquid cash; which Ordinance has not derogated the Ceremonial.

The three deputies cannot accept money, nor issue receipts the one without the other, but jointly, because this is not only denoted by those words of the ceremonial *facendosene far le quittanze dai medesimi deputati* (the receipts are made by the same deputies), but further the reason for which this decision has been made is to avoid with the presence of more people fraud and simulation, which could occur in receiving payment.

The debtor who makes the payment to others than the three deputies cannot have neither the passive vote although in the Ceremonial it says to the effect of not casting the vote; being that in case of election in the passive vote is included also the active vote. Because a Brother being elected among the 24 or among the 16 such election carries with it the active vote, that is, to vote among the said 24 or 16 as is manifest.

Chapter X

Of the Qualification to vote at the election of the Grandmaster

The Council of State ordains that every Langue or otherwise as will appear better expedient for prompt expedition, compiles a list of those Religious, who, according to the new Constitution, have the right to vote, with their name, surname, country of birth, and denomination, time of reception of the Habit, of the residence and of the caravans. *Ceremonial Cap. 3.* Usually the Priors of the Langue by order of the Council compile Langue by Langue the said list, in which, according to the order of their seniority, are described the Brethren who in conformity to the Bull have the right to vote; to be noted the day on which said seniority commenced running; the residence, which is ascertained from the registers of the Treasury; and the caravans, which are extracted from the records of the Langues. The abovestated words of the ceremonial: *the time of the reception of the Habit* do not want to denote that the time of seniority commences to run from the time of the profession because it is without doubt that it commences running from the day of the presentation in the Langue, having received the proofs and paid the fee [passaggio]; but one may believe that said words are inserted in order to see clearly that that Brother has professed in the Religion. Since the electors *de jure* have to be professed *Lezan. tom 2 cap. 25, n. 2.* And tacit profession is not sufficient, but is necessary the expressed profession in order to be elected Superior. *Lezan. tom. 1 cap. 18, n. 5.* And in the list are added the caravans, not for the ability to vote, but to know in case of parity of votes who has to precede.

The abovementioned list inserted in an Edict to be issued by the same Council is affixed publicly, so that who feels aggravated or wants to oppose against someone also of a different Langue, may produce his reasons in the records of the Vice-Chancellor or others deputized for the purpose, but not beyond the term fixed in advance by the Edict *Cerim. Cap. 3.* Who wants to oppose any exception in the Chancery it is not enough to oppose in general terms but must give specifically the reason of his opposition, which is brought to the knowledge of the Maestro Scudiere (Master Equerry) by means of a summon, so that the person against whom opposition is made may prepare his defence. One also denotes the words of the Ceremonial, whereby who wants to oppose may submit one's reasons in the records of the Vice Chancellor.

The term which the Council of State assigns in the Edict for the grievances and complaints in conformity to the Ceremonial, usually is all the time which precedes the convocation of the Council of State, in which are decided all the said matters without giving place to appeal. When the term expires one cannot oppose any sort of disqualification. Of which even before the new Bull of Urban VIII one reads a notable example in the Council of State on 7 Sept. 1622, that is, on the day of the public assembly a Brother of the Langue of Auvergne having wanted to exclude from the vote the Servant-at-Arms Caccialepre, received within limits of grace, as on the antecedent day it was decided against the chaplain Tolossenti by the Council of State. The Secret Council assembled in the vestry and decided that it could not then deal with similar incidents, which had to be dealt with on the antecedent day so that the said Caccialepre remained vested with the vote.

But talking of that disqualification, which proceeds from the debts to the Treasury, to allege prohibition must mean those debts which look for warning and condemnation and consequently altercation of the party, which is no more in time to make it, the term already assigned having expired. But debts which do not need admonition or condemnation, which are the liquid debts or of rights according to *Stat. XX e XXI Signif.* these can always be alleged, even though against the elected of the 24 or of the 16 in the same manner that is adopted in the Council, in which at all time one can allege the incapacity of the said debts, because in the Ceremonial there is nothing which diversifies this case from that; rather in this quite great rigour is shown against debtors with the election of the three deputies. However the liquid debtor or of rights must pay promptly the debt in their hands and otherwise he remains disqualified for election.

But even during the term assigned in the Edict, those exceptions of incapacity which are not promptly proved, but need a longer examination, are not decided in this judgement, which is of immediate expedition. However there being opposed the incapacity to vote to Prior of Barletta Piccolomini at the election of Grandmaster de Redin, being debtor of double responsions, for not having made the improvements of commandery in conformity to *Ordinaz. 25 Com.*, the Council of State declared him entitled to vote, both because this opposition was not notified to him within the term prefixed by the Edict and also because that debt was not adjudicated; the matter required a protracted discussion, *Consiglio 16 August 1657*. And in fact Commissioners having been deputized, the Ven. Council declared the said Prior did not incur the punishment of the double responsions for improvements not carried out, in view of the legitimate impediment of the plague, which then afflicted the realm of Naples. *Consiglio 24 October 1657*.

The dispensed in the limits (territories) outside all the Langues or of the whole Religion, be they knights or servants-at-arms, nor the chaplains who are not priests, nor the servants-at-arms received by mere grace, without having submitted the proofs cannot likewise in virtue of any privilege or grace even specially obtained from the Holy See or of custom also from time immemorial or of any other pretext, give nor receive the vote nor intrude in the proceedings relating to the election. But the Bishop of Malta and the Prior of the church, who are or will be *pro tempore* and the knights Grand Cross, although received with said dispensation have the active and passive vote in respect of the election of only the 24. Reserved are the reasons for the Bishop and for the Langue of Alemagne, if they have any *Ceremonial Cap. 3*. The prohibition from voting to the dispensed within the limits (territories) outside all the Langues is not intended for the Brethren who born in the limits of a Langue are received in another with dispensation, because they are not born outside the limits (territories) of all the Langues *Cons. 21. August 1630 and 7 May 1631*. For this reason it is restricted solely to Maltese who are received with Apostolic dispensation, because these are born outside the limits (territories) of all the Langues. To these, however, much before the

Bull of Urban VIII this prohibition was enforced by *Stat. IV Elez*. That those received by grace cannot vote in the election of the Grandmaster.

Excluded from voting are the servants-at-arms received by mere grace, but not those who submit some proof, because the ceremonial excludes from voting the servants-at-arms received by mere grace and without having submitted the proofs and as one reads more clearly in the Latin text: *ex mera gratia et nullis factis probationibus*.

Disqualified of voting are the chaplains received by grace, although the ceremonial excludes from voting only the servants-at-arms received by grace; in any case they are excluded from voting in virtue of the disposition of *Stat IV Elez*. That no one received by grace can vote at the election of the Grandmaster. It is well nigh true that it is stated in the said Statute, received by grace and not as in the ceremonial for the servants-at-arms *ex mera gratia et nullis factis probationibus*, the Council of State sometimes has decided, that a chaplain, received by grace without further proofs other than legitimacy, had voted on *10 July 1636* in favour of the Discalced chaplain, and sometimes excluded him from the vote on *4 June 1660* against chaplain Calangeli. It is however quite true that in the Briefs of those received by grace, Maltese excepted, they have almost always had the privilege to vote as if they were received by justice; and in such instance the Council always declared itself in their favour; many more such examples one comes across in the Council of State *16 August 1657*.

Not excluded from voting are the Brethren who have not made confession and received Holy Communion at the four festivities of the year, according to *Ordinaz. 29 della Chiesa*, because this does not speak of the election of the Grandmaster saying only that one loses the vote, active and passive, in the Langues, in the Councils and in the Tribunals of the Religion *Cons. Stat. 9 February 1600 ab Incarn*.

Who is not present at the General Assembly *Cons. Stat. 23 July 1690* has neither active nor passive vote, if not for being elected Grandmaster;

since the Grandmaster can be elected even being absent in conformity to *Stat. 1. Elez.*

Stat. XXVII Proibiz. disposes that the Brother accused of a crime can receive Commandery before he is found guilty, even if he is retained in imprisonment. But who is found guilty whilst undergoing punishment, before he is absolved or has fulfilled the punishment imposed on him, cannot receive Commandery, Benefice or other office of our Religion. From which Statute one deduces that if the Brother accused of any crime is not yet condemned nor imprisoned, he has active and passive vote. If he is not condemned but is kept in imprisonment he has no vote, neither active nor passive, as being absent from the General Assembly; but has only passive vote, as regards being elected Grandmaster, as mentioned before. If he is condemned and is held in prison, he loses the active and passive vote also as regards being elected Grandmaster, since the annexed *Statute XXVII Proibiz.* stipulates the disqualification to any office. If he is condemned but is not kept in prison and the period of punishment lasts (such as being condemned to pay a certain amount every year to the Treasury or being disqualified for some time from receiving Commanderies, and to similar penalties which do not carry with them imprisonment) he is disqualified of the passive vote as per annexed *Stat. XXVII Proibiz.* which excludes him from every office; but with regards the active vote, one must say, that he does not lose it. For this reason *Cons. Stat. 9 February 1600* ab Incar. decided that a Brother would be maintained in possession of the vote, notwithstanding he is still within the term of the penalty imposed on him.

Who is undergoing Settana (7 days) or Quarantena (40 days) has neither active nor passive vote, because he is considered undergoing justice, that is to say, in prison. For this reason *Stat LV Proibiz.* forbids him to come out of his house if not to go to church and attend at Divine service since attending church is the fulfilment of penitence, and not to intervene in any other function with his other Brethren; nevertheless at the election of Grandmaster Gessan whilst undergoing justice for debts Cav. Vecchi was appointed Captain of the *Captitana* and set free and consequently was enabled to vote at that election *Cons. 5 February 1659. ab Incarn.* And in the Council of State at the election of Grandmaster Perellos two Brethren who were imprisoned in the Castle [St. Angelo] were denied the vote and to another who was undergoing justice could attend public Assembly in order to vote at the election of the Grandmaster *Cons. 6 February 1696. ab Incarn.* It is quite true that at the election of Grandmaster de Redin the Council of State *Cons. Stat. 11 August 1657* granted permission to some Brethren, who were undergoing justice, to come to the church of St. John to vote, having to return to their home immediately afterwards in order to conform to justice. What I have said of the imprisoned Brethren and retained by justice proceeds also *de jure comuni* according to which such Religious should not be called to intervene at the election of their Superiors *Pelizz. Manual tract. 9, cap. 2. n. 71.*

To vote in the chapels three years of residence and having reached the age of eighteen years are necessary, precisely so many as are necessary to vote in the Langues as per *Stat. XXVIII Cons. ed Ordin 21. Proibiz.* This applies to knights and servants-at-arms because the chaplains cannot vote, if they are not priests and consequently they must have attained the age of 14 years. And although it may appear that five years of residence are necessary to have the passive vote and be elected one of the 24 or of the 16 *Stat. V. Capit.* disposes that in whatever Council or judgement of Our Order, the Brother cannot intervene, who for five continuous years or at intervals, has not resided in the Convent, excepted the Brethren of the Langues of England today Anglo-Bavarian and of Alemagne; this notwithstanding to all the Brethren irrespectively suffice only three years of residence in the Convent, besides the other capacity, in order thus to have at the election of the Grandmaster the active vote in the chapels for electing the three electors as to have the passive vote and be elected one of the 24 or of the 16.

The privileges which the Ceremonial preserves to the Langue of Alemagne at the election of the Grandmaster are reduced only to the proviso of residence; since *Stat. V. Capit.* requires that the Brethren of the Langue of Alemagne can vote in the Chapter General and in the Councils also when they do not have the necessary residence. And *Stat. XXVIII Cons*. disposes that the Brethren of the said Langue can vote in the Langue even though they do not have the three-year residence. The observance is that to them it is sufficient to have made the regular profession to vote in all the nominated Tribunals. But apart from this question of residence, the Brethren of Alemagne are subject to all the disqualifications prescribed in the Ceremonial and to any other, and especially to that *of Ordinaz. 11 Proibiz*. that the Brethren cannot vote in the Langue if they have not attained the age of 18 years.

And no doubt, the electors have to be free from canonical censure and impediments and those excommunicated with major excommunication cannot be elected. And according to some authors neither the irregulars *Lezzan questa Regul*. But the Council of State on *10 June 1596* declared that a priest although irregular could vote. There is doubt however if someone who is disobedient, I say, excommunicated, whether he does not annul the election but is admitted to vote with the premise of such doubt, being that no doubtful matters enjoy possession *Lezzan doc. cit. n. 7*. Who has not resided for three years in the Convent cannot vote at the election of the Grandmaster, even though provided with Apostolic dispensation or commanderies *Cons. Stat. 1 February 1660 ab Incarn*.

According to chapter three of the Ceremonial those disqualified to vote cannot even assist at the proceedings concerning the election. For this reason they are excluded from intervening in the General Assembly. But since the Ceremonial in *cap. 5* says that all the Religious may assembly on the usual day in the church of St. John, and then every one of those who has the vote goes in the chapel of his Langue; nevertheless those disqualified to vote, although they can intervene in the church of St. John, according to the Ceremonial *cap. 5* cannot however assist at the proceedings concerning the election, according to the Ceremonial *cap. 3*. And nevertheless a Maltese chaplain, Secretary of the Chancery, could not be substituted in place of the Vice Chancellor, elected among the 21 at the election of the Most Eminent Perellos.

Chapter XI

The Duties of the Council of State when the Magisterium is vacant

The Council of State at the nomination of each elector, infirm or in any other way justly hindered to write, deputizes those, who in their stead will have to write their names, surnames and ceremonial denominations *cap. 4.* This is meant for those who are infirm or in any other way are hindered from writing, who can actually be present in the public assembly and not of those who cannot be present. *Cons. Stat. 23 July 1690.*

Moreover the Council of State decides summarily, without any form of judgement, also by Royal hand, in conformity however to the Statutes and usages of the Religion, remote every appeal, complete restitution or any thing else, which may delay the execution, all the lawsuits relating to the said grievances and exceptions and any other controversy also of the 24 or of the 16, until the election of the Grandmaster has been completed *Ceremonial cap. 4.*

Those elected among the 24 or among the 16 cannot enter the Council of State, if it happens to assemble. As regards the 16 it is most certain: because once locked up in conclave for the election of the Grandmaster, it is inappropriate to have contact with others of the Assembly. For this reason *Stat. 1 Elez.* disposes that the 16 having been elected immediately without talking to any one for whatsoever reason and without disclosing anything by gesture or by sign, they leave the Assembly etc. and enter in Conclave; and the doors are closed in such manner that no one else can enter therein etc. and as regards the 24 neither do they intervene therein; and this was the case at the election of Grandmaster Gessan *9 February 1659 ab Incarn.* in which after the election of the three in many Langues the Council of State was convened because of a doubt that had arisen for the nomination of one of the three for the Langue of Italy. And in such instances the Councillors already elected among the 24 or among the 16 others are substituted in conformity to what is practised in the Council.

In case of any controversy the Council of State assembles in the Oratory of St. John in terms of decree of the *Consigli di Stato 4 June 1660.*

Chapter XII

The General Assembly, the Oath of the Brethren and the Nomination of the three Electors by each Langue

At dawn of the following day at the convocation of the Council of State all the Brethren assemble in the church of St. John (all those forming the Ordinary Council are advised to wear the Manto di Punta [the Habit]) and after Mass and the hymn *Veni Creator Spiritus,* those who are entitled to vote go in the chapel of their Langue; the Brethren of the Langue of the Lieutenant remain in the main vault of the church *Ceremonial cap. 1.*

Although at first the Lieutenant, seated in the middle of the church, delivers a short exhortation to the Bailiffs, Priors and Seniors, ordained to sit for the election of a most worthy Grandmaster. And then he commands that all the Brethren, who will be voting, retire in the chapels of their Langues *Stat. 1 Elez.*

The Brethren having retired in the chapel of their Langue must elect by secret vote not one, as was previously customary, but three Brother Knights each Langue, capable and qualified according to the Ceremonial and the Statutes, in such manner that not eight Brother Knights, as previously, are elected, but twenty four *Ceremonial Cap. 5.*

Instead of one for each Langue nowadays three are elected, so that the most influential in the Langues do not exclude totally the less influential, who perhaps will have more upright intention. And for the same purpose there is only one scrutiny for the election of the said three for each Langue, because if there is one scrutiny for each one the most influential would elect all three of the Langue.

Among the 21 can be elected Knights Grand Cross although *Stat. 1 Elez.* and the *Ceremonial cap. 5.* want that they are Brother Knights *Cons. Stat. 10 July 1503.* Item the Knights of Grace, who before were Servants-at-arms, who however cannot be elected to the Triumvirate. *Consiglio di Stato 10 June 1636.* Item the Lieutenant of the Magisterium *Ceremonial cap. 6.* as was the case at the election of Grandmaster Lascaris *10 June 1636* and at the election of Grandmaster Cottoner First [Rafael] *4 June 1660.* Although a long time ago this was prohibited, that the Assembly would not remain without a Head *Cons. Stat 17 June 1476.* Item among the 21 can be elected the Bishop and the Prior of the church, although the electors have to be Brother Knights according to the Ceremonial *cap. 5.* Since in another place the same Ceremonial, that is, in Chapter 3, requires that the Bishop and the Prior of the church and any other Knight Grand Cross, although received with grace of limits (territories) outside all the Langues, may be elected among the 24.

The ballot-papers should be impressed or written by the same hand as per specimen hereunder:

> I Fra N
> elect Fra N
> as one of the 24

And placed on a table in the chapels and the main nave of the above-mentioned church respectively, each elector goes to the said table alone and separately, the others standing afar, and writes in the upper part of the ballot-paper the name, surname, denomination of the person to be elected, in a manner that it is clear who is the person electing and the person to be elected, and in his own handwriting, otherwise the vote is invalid, excepted the dispensed who can write through a third person and nominating not more than one for each ballot-paper, as per specimen hereunder:

> I Fra Silvestro Scoto
> Elect Fra Niccolo' La Marra
> as one of the 24.

And the scrutiny is repeated until three are elected for each Langue. *Ceremonial cap. 5.*

Each elector folds the ballot-paper at the upper part and seals it with the common seal of the Langue and in a manner that the name of the person electing cannot be seen. Then he folds the whole ballot-paper in a manner that therefore it cannot be read by anyone. Then he takes the said ballot-paper and raising it at the tip of his fingers in a manner that publicly it is shown to be only one, he will swear in a loud and intelligible voice in the following manner:

> I NN swear to elect that who according to God I consider should be elected.

Which oath is renewed in all the elections to be made in virtue of the new Bull, and then he puts back the ballot-paper in the vase prepared for the purpose on the same table. *Ceremonial cap. 5.* By which form of oath ceased the disposition of *Stat 1 Elez.* that the Brethren before assembling in their chapels take the oath in the presence of the Lieutenant and of the Assembly to elect a Brother of their Langue there present sufficient and worthy for election of Commendatore of the Election and of the Triumvirate.

The Brethren cannot carry arms at the place of the election of the Grandmaster. Who contravenes is forthwith deprived of the vote, and if he queries, he loses the Habit *Stat. 11 Elez.* which prohibition applies also for defensive arms, because *de jure* by the name arms are meant those offensive as well as those defensive. *Barbos de Diction verb. Ama 25.*

In conformity to which the *Cons. di Stat 9 February 1600 ab Incarn* ordained that in the next Assembly nobody should carry arms, offensive
or defensive, of whatsoever nature.

Chapter XIII

The three Scrutinizers

This having been done, three knights, the most senior, without regard to
preemeinence, besides the other duties, which are assigned them as
scrutinizers, must count openly and publicly the ballot-papers placed in
the urn, in a manner that all the electors can see and hear. And in case
the ballot-papers do not tally with the number of electors they are
burned incontinent and in public. A scrutiny is repeated until the number of ballot-papers tallies with the number of electors. And then the
scrutinizers reading the ballot-papers in the unsealed part make public
the person who is elected by the said ballot-papers, *Ceremonial cap. 6*.

Those three knights are considered elected in each Langue that have the
majority of votes; provided each has obtained at least one fourth, *Ceremonial cap. 6*. In counting the fourth part of the necessary votes to be
elected as one of the three for each Langue, no account is taken of those
votes which do not have the fourth part without fraction, that is, which
cannot be divided in four parts. And however 18 is the fourth part of 74,
because although 18 multiplied by 4 makes 72 thus are advanced 2
votes; these do not have the fourth part without fraction, which must not
be admitted in the counting of votes, *Cons. di Stat 9 Febr 1659 ab Incarn*.

If none or two or only one of the three to be elected will have had this
fourth part of the votes, the scrutiny is repeated as many times in respect
of the others who have not obtained the fourth part, until the three are
elected with the said fourth part, *Ceremonial cap. 6*.

The person elected with only the necessary votes must acknowledge his own ballot-paper and show that he has not voted for himself; which he cannot do. And refusing to acknowledge or show it, he is considered in that case not elected. The elected is excluded from voting for the non-elected, and enters immediately in conclave, *Ceremonial cap. 6.*

The votes cannot be neither uncertain, such as would be, I elect him whom Giovanni wants, nor alternative, as would be, I elect Pietro or Giovanni; neither can the votes be left blank, because in such instances, also if the Brother refuses openly to vote, such ballot-papers are not counted with the others. *Lezan 99 Regul tom 1. cap. 15 n. 16 & 18.* At the election of Grandmaster Lascaris some Brethren of the Langue of Aragon having refused to vote at the election for the fourth for the Langue of England, the Maestro Scudiere (Master Equerry) on order of the Lieutenant intimated the said Brethren that they had to vote, otherwise the other Brethren in their absence would have proceeded with the termination of the scrutiny *Cons. di Stat 12 June 1636.*

At the election of Grandmaster Wignacourt the Second [Adrien] one voted by seniority in the Langue of Italy and not by preeminence, although there was in that Langue the Lieutenant; likewise in that of Aragon, but not in that of Provence. And in the other Langues the preemenences were the seniors, and in that of Italy and numerous other Langues one voted two at a time, to shorten the duration of the election.

The three for each Langue having been elected each Pilier thereupon informs the Lieutenant. Before whom each one of the three elected, one after the other, takes the two oaths: the first one for the election of the President of the election, and the second for the election of the Triumvirate, *Cons. di Stat. 24 July 1690.* Each one having done this, he enters immediately in conclave in conformity with the Ceremonial.

If the Lieutenant is elected from among the three for each Langue, another Lieutenant is deputized immediately or the most senior of the same Council, there present, without taking regard of preeminence, presides instead of the Lieutenant, as appears expedient to the Council, *Ceremonial Cap. 6.*

In such case the Lieutenant convenes the Council of State for the election of a successor, who, being elected, takes in the hands of the Lieutenant, as that, who still exercises the lieutenancy, the usual oath. And then he takes the chair, *Cons. di Stat. 10 June 1636.* At the election of Grandmaster Cotoner the First [Rafael] being Marshal Arfugliers, Lieutenant to the Magisterium, elected one of the three and deputized in his stead the Prior of Messina Balbiani, the Langue of Auvergne persisting in the main nave of the church, where the election had commenced, appointed the fourth for the Langue of England, *Cons. di Stat. 4 June 1660.*

Chapter XIV

The President of the Election and the Triumvirate

The twenty-four having been elected they enter in conclave, in which the election of the Grandmaster is necessarily carried out - as I shall better explain in *chapter II and IVI.*

Firstly, they elect with the said oath the President of the Election by secret vote according to the old usage up to now adopted by the Convent *Ceremonial, cap. 8.,* which usage is described in *Stat. 1 Elez.,* and its contents is as follows.

Having elected the eight Brethren (who nowadays are twenty-four), these take the oath before the Vicegerente for the election of a Brother Knight of all the Assembly or of them as Commendatore (President) of the Election; and then in conclave they elect him by scrutiny of votes (and in everything conforming to the election of the latter described above in chapter two), and he is made known to the Assembly by their Preeminent. And the elected Commendatore takes the oath in the hand of the Lieutenant to exercise correctly his office; and the Lieutenant relinquishes his office, whilst the former presides, in front of whom the eight electors (who nowadays are the 24) vow to elect a Knight, a Chaplain and a Servant-at-arms as electors of their other companions, electioneers of the Grandmaster. And the same oath is taken also by the Commendatore of the Election in the hand of the Lieutenant, if he is one of the eight electioneers, that is, of the 24, and otherwise remaining in the Assembly he presides *Stat. 1. Elez.* and performs all those things which the Presidents of the Election should and can do by reason, privilege, usage and custom, with the abovementioned prohibition of granting favours and other things forbidden to him *Cerimon. Cap. 8.*

The Commendatore of the Election takes his seat on the right of the Lieutenant *Cons. Stat. 22 November 1512.* But if he is one of the 24 having taken the oath in the hand of the Lieutenant with the other 23, his companions, and with them had retired in conclave, for the election of the Triumvirate, as aforesaid, the Lieutenant continues to preside *Stat. I. Elez.* until he is informed that the Triumvirate has been elected; and therefore deposing his office, surrenders his right hand to the Commendatore of the Election and takes his seat on his left, *Cons. di Stat. 22, November 1512.* This procedure was followed at the election of Grandmaster Mendez, *Cons. 17 September 1622* and at the election of Grandmaster de Paule *Cons. 9 March 1622 ab Incarn.*

If as Commendatore of the Election is elected the Lieutenant, he takes the usual oath in the hand of the most preeminant *Cons. 12 June 1626.*

The Commendatore of the Election, if the elected Grandmaster is absent, stays until the Complete Council has elected his Vicegerente according to *Stat. 1. Elez. Cons. 23 November 1535.*

Secondly, the 24 with the same oath elect the Triumvirate, that is, a Knight, a Chaplain and a Servant-at-arms, who may be of diverse Langues, with the scrutiny of the ballot-papers aforesaid *Cerimonial Cap. 9.*

The three Brethren of the Triumvirate need not be of diverse nations, since the Ceremonial only mentions that they may be of diverse Langues. And the same is explained by *Stat. 1. Elez.* by those words; they elect the fourth of other Langues other than theirs. This was the case at the election of Grandmaster de Redin: the Knight was from Provence, the Chaplain, French, and the Servant-at-arms, Portuguese *Cons. 17 August 1657.*

At the election of the Triumvirate the same procedure is followed as at the election of the President of the Election, since the Ceremonial says: with the scrutiny of the ballot-papers abovementioned, that is, as immediately said above, where it deals with the election of the Commendatore of the Election, who is elected by only one scrutiny for all the proposed candidates and with the plurality of votes. And since the first to be elected is the Knight so that so many ballot-papers are put as are nominated Knights of Election by the 24 electors, who are generally two. And proceeding with only one scrutiny, that candidate is considered elected who obtains the plurality of votes. This is what those words want to say, which in the registers of the Councils record at their election: *cum suffr. scr. per singulars adhibito.* And in like manner then one proceeds with the election of the Chaplain, and finally with that of the Servant-at-arms. But the election is not made public in the Assembly (by the Preeminent among the 24 electors) for all three may not be elected in conformity with *Stat. 1 Elez.* It is quite true that there being no opposition, only one scrutiny would suffice for all the Triumvirate. And one sole scrutiny would also suffice if there is opposition to all the Triumvirate for the one and for the other part.

The Knight of the Election can be elected from among the 24. Because at the election of Grandmaster de Paule, Fra Christoph Abandlau, Lieutenant of the Grand Bailiff, who was one of the eight electors, was then nominated Knight of the Election, *Cons. 9 March 1622 ab Incarn.* And the same can be said of the other 13, who can be elected from among the 24, as has happened several times. And the *Ceremonial Cap. 10* requires that if there is discrepancy among the Triumvirate in electing the fourth, three Knights must be nominated so that one of these is elected as the fourth from among the 24, even though he forms part of the 24. Although he may not to be a Knight Grand Cross, as I shall explain in the following chapter. For this reason not even the Bishop, and the Prior of the church, can be elected as Chaplain of the Election, as I shall better explain in the same chapter.

But the 24 electors have to remain standing up till the completion of the election of the fourth of the 16 electioneers, as I shall explain in the following chapter; nevertheless happening to elect the Knight of the Election from among the 24, it is believed, that in such case a new candidate must be elected in the Langue, to which the Knight of the Election belongs, or at least following the case of discrepancy of the Triumvirate in the election of the fourth, with which I shall deal soon.

Although the Knights of Grace, who before were Servants-at-arms, can be elected among the 21, they cannot however be elected as Knights of the Election, *Cons. di Stat. 10 June 1636.*

The Triumvirate having been elected, the preeminent among the 24 informs the Assembly thereof; and the three who are elected immediately take the oath in the hand of the Commendatore of the Election Stat. *Stat. 1 Elez.*, that is, electing according to God their other 13 companions and admonished by the said Commendatore briefly of their office and commands them that no one speaks to them; they enter in the conclave, where there are the 24 electors.

Chapter XV

The Election of the Thirteen other Electors and Procedure to be followed in case of parity of votes in the Election

The three Brethren of the Triumvirate must elect unanimously a fourth one of different Langue from theirs, *Ceremonial Cap. 10.*

And not agreeing on a candidate within the space of an hour to commence from the first moment of the closure of the conclave, each one of them nominates another Knight, who appears a better one to each of them, *Ceremonial Cap. 10.* All three Brethren of the Triumvirate must agree on one candidate, otherwise they nominate three Knights; and that two may agree is not enough, because the Ceremonial requires that the three unanimously elect the fourth.

These three nominated Brethren have to be of three Langues different from those of the three Brethren of the Triumvirate, *Ceremonial Cap. 10.* Because it is not enough that each of the three nominates a candidate different from his own Langue, but must be different from the Langue of all the three of them, because the first eight electioneers of the Grandmaster must all be of a different Langue, excepted if one of the said Triumvirate wanted to nominate as fourth one of the Langue of England, because in such case one would think that one can nominate a candidate of all the Brethren capable of the Assembly of any Langue.

Of the three aforesaid nominated Brethren the 24 retire in the vestry assigned to them only in this case instead of the conclave, and with the said oath they elect one by secret ballot and each one of them casts his vote, on the understanding that elected as fourth that who will obtain the higher number of votes in respect to the minor one, *Ceremonial Cap. 10.*

The election of the Grandmaster must take place in the same conclave in which are assembled the 24 electors, which is a room beneath the belfry, and before it was the vestry, not far away from every outside contact. The *Ceremonial Cap. 8* says: "The 24 having been elected, they go to the place of the conclave, in which must necessarily take place the election of the Grandmaster". Nevertheless the three of the Triumvirate having been elected, they retire in the same conclave, as laid down by the *Ceremonial Cap. 10* leaving then the 24. But there arising the need that these have to elect the fourth because of disagreement of the Triumvirate, and not being able to carry out comfortably this election in the same conclave in the presence of the Triumvirate, the Ceremonial assigns to them the vestry only in this case instead of the conclave.

This election of the fourth which is carried out by voting for each of the three nominated candidates, is meant by voting for all three together with a voting-box for each in conformity to *Stat. XVIII Cons.* as I explained above at *Cap. I.*

The said fourth can be elected from among the 24 *Ceremonial Cap. 10.*

The fourth thus elected together with the other three, elects in like manner the fifth. And the fifth similarly elected together with the other four, elects the sixth by the majority of votes, and so on succeessively up to the number of sixteen of each Langue, according to their preemeninences as observed up to now, *Ceremonial Cap. 10.*

The eight having been elected, the others, up to the number of 16, are elected in the order of the Langues *Stat. 1. Elez.*

The said election is made with two voting-boxes, if there is only one candidate; one for *ayes* and the other for *no*. And if the nominated candidates are two or more, with corresponding number of voting-boxes; voting for all together, considered elected who obtains the plurality of votes in conformity with *Stat. XV Cons.* reproduced above at *Cap. 1.*

The election of each one of them is made known to the Assembly by the Knight of the Triumvirate; and the fourth takes the oath before the

Commendatore (President) of the Election for the election of the fifth; and the fifth for the election of the sixth, and so of the others *Stat. 1 Elez.* Excepted is the sixteenth, who has no motive to take the oath as there are no others to be elected.

The fourth not agreeing with the election of the fifth some opine that one must make the same one, who in the election of the fourth, that is, all four not being in agreement as regards a candidate, they nominate four knights in compliance with the above words of the Ceremonial, that the fourth so elected with the other three elects equally the fifth, almost that those words, so elected, and those other words, *elects equally the fifth (elegge parimente il quinto)* may denote that the election of the fifth must be made, like that of the fourth, as seem to denote again the following words: *And the fifth similarly elected (ed il quinto similmente eletto).*

So much so that the Ceremonial passing to the election of the sixth changes form of words adding: "and the fifth similarly elected with other four proceeds with the election of the sixth by majority of votes." Other authors, and more justly think, that having completed the election of the fourth, one may proceed with the election of the others up to the number of 16 by plurality of votes, requiring that those words *equally (parimente)* and *similarly (similmente)* do not denote *similitude (similitudine)* with the form of the election of the fourth, but continuation of the election up to the number of 16 almost that one may say: "the fourth with the three elects equally the fifth". The fifth with the four elects equally the sixth, by majority of votes; and so on up to the election of the sixteenth, concluding that if the Bull would have intended otherwise, it would have used words much more clearly in a matter of so much importance. That if in this election there occurs parity of votes, one follows what is explained at the end of the present chapter.

If any Langue for lack of Brethren cannot supply this number of two, these are elected from another Langue, *Stat. 1. Elez.* that is, by the colleague electors, because with them rests the election up to the number of sixteen; and they elect them of any Langue as they decide. And thus there being lack of Brethren in the Langue of England, a Poruguese and a German were elected *Cons. 9 March 1622 ab Incarn*. And on another occasion an Italian and an Aragonese *Cons. 17 September 1622*.

Those elected among the 16 must all be born of legitimate wedlock, but none is Knight Grand Cross, and there can be amongst them two Chaplains and three Servants-at-arms, and not more, and at least a Chaplain and a Servant-at-arms. *Stat. 1 Elez*. But according to the Ceremonial only one Chaplain and one Servant-at-arms are admitted in the election of the Triumvirate as explained in the preceding chapter. And excluded the Knights Grand Cross, all the others must be Knights. This is gleaned from the Ceremonial at Cap. 20 reproduced above: "that the Triumvirate not agreeing in the election of the fourth, each one of them may nominate in that case another Brother Knight." And this has always been the custom since the new Constitution todate.

Neither the Bishop nor the Prior of the church can be elected as Chaplain of the Election, because from the number of the 16 electors is excluded any Knight Grand Cross as per *Stat. 1 Elez*. and expressly the Bishop and the Prior of the church as *per Ceremonial Cap. 3*. Contrary is the example of the Prior of the church Papefust, elected as Chaplain of the Triumvirate at the exaltation of Grandmaster Aubusson, *Cons. 17 June 1476*. Because the prohibition that among the 16 there cannot be any Knight Grand Cross was introduced later, that is, at the Chapter General held in 1558 as stated in *Stat. 1. Elez*.

The Sixteen use to sit and vote in the order of their election, without regard to seniority or preeminence, being logical that in this function the electors are preferred to the elected.

In all the above mentioned elections there occurring parity of votes, the most senior is preferred; in parity of seniority, who has longer residence in the Convent or who has held more posts in the service of the Religion for which service one has resided in the Convent to the said effect. And in parity of residence, who has made the more caravans, *Ceremonial Cap. 10*.

Chapter XVI

The Sixteen Electors at the Election of the Grandmaster

The sixteen electors putting aside whatsoever animosity, love or any other form of human affection and having taken the oath in the form aforesaid, proceed with the election of the Grandmaster, in the person of that, whom they consider capable and suitable for the dignity and service of such an Order, as has been the case up to now. *Ceremonial Cap 11.* Which observance is described in *Stat. 1 Elez.* as follows.

The Knight of the Election in order to avoid the parity of votes at the election of the Grandmaster has two votes and presides among the 16 *Stat. 1 Elez.* By proposing only two candidates among the 16, thereby is avoided the parity with the two votes of the Knight of the Election, as is evident. But proposing more than two candidates, parity is not always avoided with the said two votes. And thus voting for three candidates A, B, C , it could happen that A obtains six votes, B six votes and C five votes, and thus A and B are at par and this parity has not avoided the two votes of the Knight of the Election. But as this case will perhaps never occur, just as it is not known whether it has happened up to now, that is, that more than two candidates have been proposed among the 16 electors; nevertheless the Statute assigned two votes to the Knight of the Election in order to avoid parity, having regard to the things which more commonly used to happen.

The sixteen electors by order of the Commendator (President) of the Election confess, hear Mass and receive Holy Communion *Stat. 1 Elez.* The omission of confession and Holy Communion does not invalidate the election, since there is no irritating clause in *Stat. 1 Elez.* Neither the Bull does dispose anything new in this regard. And although *de Jure Canonico* some authors think, that it is required as an essential part of the election the Mass of the Holy Spirit and confession and Holy Communion; others however conclude to the contrary, *Castellin. de Elect. Cap. 3 n. 2.* It is well nigh true that this usage has always been observed at the election of grandmasters, excepted if sometimes the election of the 16 has not been conclusive, after the lapse of many hours after midday, in which case the 16 electors did not confess and receive Holy Communion, *Cons. 22 November 1511* and *15 December 1513* but heard low Mass. But at the election of Grandmaster Lascaris the 16 neither heard the Mass of the Holy Spirit nor could they receive Holy Communion, because two hours of the night had elapsed, and the majority of them had out of necessity taken food, *Cons. 12 June 1636*. The same thing happened in the following elections of Grandmaster de Redin *Cons. 17 August 1657* and of Grandmaster Gessan *9 February 1659 ab Incarn.*

Then the 16 electors take the oath one by one before the Commendatore of the Election or all the Assembly on the Holy Cross, on the Holy Gospels and on the Preface of the Mass, to elect a Knight absent or present, born of legitimate wedlock, suitable, good, virtuous, sufficient and capable of the Magisterium, *Stat. 1 Elez.* The 16 electors take the oath one by one, first the Knight of the Election, then the Chaplain, then the Servant-at-arms and then the others according to the order of their nomination, which oath is taken by all the councillors, sitting in the benches near the President of the Election.

The qualities which must be present in a candidate to be worthily elected to the Magisterium, are the following: first, be a Brother Knight of the same Religion *Stat. III. Maest. Stat. I. Elez.* and *Ceremonial Cap. 12.* Second, be born of legitimate wedlock *Stat. III. Maest.* and *Stat. I. Elez.;* third, not being received by grace of limits *Cerem. Cap. 12.* The Latin text says : *de alio, quam uno ex Fratibus Militibus ex eadem limitum gratia nequaquam receptis:* that is, not received with grace of limits outside all the Langues, because the Ceremonial in the same chapter 12 previously disposes, that at the election of the Grandmaster must precede the election of three Brethren Knights of each Langue, not received with grace of limits, according to the manner and form aforementioned. Which form was declared by the Ceremonial *Cap. 3* where it disposes that disqualified to vote or to receive a vote any Brother born outside the (territories) of all the Langues or of all the Religion, with which he may be dispensed over the defects of the limits. Fourth, the candidate has to be suitable, good, virtuous, sufficient and capable of the Magisterium *Stat. 1. Elez.* and *Ceremonial Cap. 11*. Fifth, not having any canonical impediment and principally not being excommunicated, not being heretic nor son of an heretic up to the second generation on the paternal side and up to the first generation on the maternal side. *A bononia de election. dub. 82, Pelliz. tract. 9, cap. 2. n. 172 & seq.* And finally not having procured the Magisterium by illicit means, that is to say, by ambitious agreements or by simony.

Ambitions agreements render the election null *de jure Canonico. A Bononia de elect. dub. 56. n. 1* and in our Order they are punished even by privation of the Habit, thus the Brethren, who for themselves or for others ask for votes at the election to any dignity, status, or office, similarly the electors if they promise such votes in any manner *Ordinaz. 2 Elez.*

Ambitious agreements are prohibited when these derive from depraved affection for exalting the undeserving candidate, in such manner that the community receives therefrom evident harm, but not when they derive from upright intention to represent merit and to promote a worthy candidate for the common good, *Castellin de Elect. cap. 3, n. 6. Pelliz. tract. 9. cap. 2. n. 20.*

Simony renders the election null, and leads to various penalties *de jure canonico*, meaning however not mental simony, which stops at the sole intention, nor the conventional, which consists of an accord between the parties, without giving anything in return, but the real, that is, when said consignment follows *Pelliz loc. cit. n. 67.* But about this subject see *Diana parte 4. tract. 4 resol. 156.*

As Grandmaster it suffices to elect a candidate worthy, leaving out the most worthy. Because the oath, which the 16 electors make, is that of electing a Brother Knight born of legitimate wedlock, suitable, good, virtuous, sufficient, capable of the Magisterium. And in the *Ceremonial Cap. 11* it is stated that the 16 electors come to electing as Grandmaster that whom they will judge capable and suitable for the dignity and utility of such Order, since neither the Statute nor the Ceremonial seeks the election of the candidate most worthy, omitted that, who nevertheless is worthy. And generally is probable the opinion that suffices to elect a worthy candidate, without the need to elect the most worthy, *Castell. de Elect. cap. 9. n. 33. Pelliz. tract. 9. cap. 2. a n. 104.*

Ordinary knights can also be elected Grandmasters, since neither by the Statutes nor by the Ceremonial are they excluded and can also be elected of the number of the 16 electors; because neither the Statutes nor the Ceremonial prohibit this. On the Contrary, in the oath which the said 16 take for the election of the Grandmaster, they say that they have to elect one from among all the knights both absent and present. And *de jure Canonico* the Superior can be elected from anong the Commissioners, *Pelliz. loc. cit. n. 10.* Also in our Order there is the famous example of Fra Deodato di Gozone, who being Knight of the Election, proposed himself to the electors, and he was elected Grandmaster, *Bosio Part. 2 lib. 2. ann. 1346.* On the contrary he was then Knight Grand Cross; it being that also private knights could be promoted to such dignity, as I said hereinbefore.

The Sixteen Electors (Sedici Elettori) having taken the above oath, then the Commendatore (President) of the Election and all the assembly swear to accept as Grandmaster him, whom the 16 will elect. Who, having retired in conclave without saying a word or making a sign to anyone, and having placed as many voting-boxes as there are proposed candidates, as is ordained to do in Council, and having discussed together of their qualities, virtues and faults, by secret ballot with plurality of votes, they elect the Grandmaster *Stat. I Elez.* Those words: "as is ordained to do in Council" denote the usage introduced by having as many voting-boxes as are the competitors, as is stated by *Stat. XVIII Consiglio.*

The 16 who have elected the Grandmaster move up (to the balustrades which mean the church) in front of the Commendatore of the Election and of the Assembly, and requested for three times, if they consider definite, that which they have done, and replying thrice in the affirmative, then the Knight of the Election announces the Grandmaster, who, if he is present, proceeds to the high altar, and on the book of Statutes swears solemnly to observe the Rule, the Establishments and the good customs of the Religion, and to govern with the Council of the Primates and of the seniors. And if he is absent, when he comes in the Convent, he takes the same oath before he enjoys any magistral preeminence, and during his absence the Council elects a Vicegerente *Stat. 1. Elez.*

Chapter XVII

The invalidity of the Election of the Grandmaster

The election of the Grandmaster is null and void and irritates *eo ipso* and should not have any effect, if any one of the following four requisites is lacking: first, if it is held otherwise than in conclave; second, if it is not preceded by the election of the three Brother Knights of each Langue, not received by grace of limits, according to the manner and form afore-said, both as regards the scrutiny and the votes; third, if it is not preceded by the election of the Triumvirate, as mentioned above, which proceeds up to the election of the 16th, that is, two for each Langue, as aforesaid, and that the election of the Grandmaster proceeds from the 16 so elected; fourth, and finally, if it follows in a manner that of one of the Brother Knights is not received by grace of limits, *Ceremonial Cap. 12*, that is, outside all the Langues, as I stated in the antecedent chapter.

The election of the Grandmaster is rendered *eo ipso* null and void as a result of the non-observance solely of the aforesaid four requisites, be-cause the Ceremonial makes mention only of these in declaring invalid *eo ipso* the aforesaid election. But for the non-observance of the other requisites contained in the Ceremonial, in the Statutes and in the Sacred Canons, the election is disallowed from having effect, subject to the pen-alties which the Pope will judge proper, who may condemn or declare null and void the election. The words which follow in the concluding part of the same Ceremonial do not oppose this: "in virtue whereof we approve and confirm perpetually all the things and each one of them ordained in the present Ceremonial, and in whatsoever manner therein contained; and to all those things and to each one of them we add the force of a perpetual and inviolable Apostolic firmness; and we ordain and command expressly to all and to each of the Brethren of the said Hospital, on whom it is enjoined, and according to time in whatsoever manner it will become encumbent that inviolably they will observe it".

Because such words do not declare the election null and void *eo ipso*, the Ceremonial being violated in other requisites, other than in the four requisites aforementioned. For this reason in case of violation of the said other requisites only the Pope can impose the penalty, which he deems appropriate.

The election of the Grandmaster does not require Apostolic sanction, because this is not laid down neither in the Ceremonial nor in the Statutes; and universally no Apostolic sanction is required at the election of the Generals of those Religious Orders, which have the privilege from the Pope to elect their Generals *Pellizz. tract. 9. cap. 2. n. 41.*, as is the case with our Religion; to which is conceded by the Statutes, confirmed by the Holy See, the faculty to elect the Grandmaster, who however after his election is installed immediately in his office and commences to administer; by which deeds he fulfils the election, without any further Apostolic confirmation, *Lotther de Re Benefic. lib 2 quast. 18. n. 39. Oldrad. Cons. 146. n. 5.*

PART III

BOLLETTINO UFFICIALE

DEL SOVRANO MILITARE ORDINE OSPEDALIERO
DI SAN GIOVANNI DI GERUSALEMME, DI RODI E DI MALTA

Numero Speciale   **Palazzo Magistrale - 68, via Condotti - Roma**   12 Gennaio 1998

CARTA COSTITUZIONALE
promulgata il 27 giugno 1961
riformata dal Capitolo Generale Straordinario del 28/30 aprile 1997

Titolo 1

L'ORDINE E SUA NATURA

Art. 1
Origine e natura dell'Ordine

Parag. 1 - Il Sovrano Militare Ordine Ospedaliero dei Cavalieri di San Giovanni di Gerusalemme, detto di Rodi, detto di Malta, sorto dal gruppo degli Ospitalari dell'Ospedale di San Giovanni di Gerusalemme, chiamato dalle circostanze ad aggiungere ai primitivi compiti assistenziali un'attività militare per la difesa dei pellegrini della Terra Santa e della civiltà cristiana in Oriente, sovrano, successivamente, nelle isole di Rodi e poi di Malta, è un Ordine religioso laicale, tradizionalmente militare, cavalleresco e nobiliare.

Parag. 2 - L'organizzazione nel territorio delle Nazioni in cui, in virtù di diritti o di convenzioni internazionali, l'Ordine esercita la sua attività, comprende Gran Priorati, Priorati, Sottopriorati e Associazioni nazionali.

Parag. 3 - Nella presente Carta e nel Codice il Sovrano Militare Ordine di Malta è detto "Ordine di Malta" ovvero "Ordine".

Parag. 4 - Nelle norme che seguono i Gran Priorati e le Associazioni nazionali sono detti Priorati e Associazioni. Il Codice Melitense è detto Codice.

Art. 2
Finalità

Parag. 1 - In ossequio alle secolari tradizioni, l'Ordine ha il fine di promuovere la gloria di Dio mediante la santificazione dei membri, il servizio alla Fede e al Santo Padre e l'aiuto al prossimo.

Parag. 2 - Fedele ai precetti divini ed ai consigli di Nostro Signore Gesù Cristo, guidato dagli insegnamenti della Chiesa, l'Ordine afferma e diffonde le virtù cristiane di carità e di fratellanza, esercitando, senza distinzione di religione, di razza, di provenienza e di età, le opere di misericordia verso gli ammalati, i bisognosi e le persone prive di patria.
In modo particolare esercita l'attività istituzionale nel campo ospedaliero, inclusa l'assistenza sociale

CONSTITUTIONAL CHARTER AND CODE OF THE SOVEREIGN MILITARY HOSPITALLER ORDER OF ST. JOHN OF JERUSALEM OF RHODES AND OF MALTA

This free translation is not be intended as a modification of the Italian text approved by the Extraordinary Chapter General 28-30 April 1997 and published in the *Bollettino Ufficiale* 12 January 1998.

In cases of different interpretations, the official Italian text prevails (Art. 36, par. 3 Constitutional Charter) .

CONSTITUTIONAL CHARTER OF THE SOVEREIGN MILITARY HOSPITALLER ORDER OF ST. JOHN OF JERUSALEM OF RHODES AND OF MALTA

promulgated 27 June 1961
revised by the Extraordinary Chapter General 28-30 April 1997

INDEX

Title IV
THE ORGANIZATION OF THE ORDER

Title I
THE ORDER AND ITS NATURE

Article 1
Origin and Nature of the Order
Par. 1 — The Sovereign Military and Hospitaller Order of the Knights of Saint John of Jerusalem, of Rhodes, and of Malta, arose from a group of hospitallers of the Hospice of Saint John of Jerusalem who had been called upon by circumstances to augment their original charitable enterprise with military service for the defence of pilgrims to the Holy Land and of Christian civilization in the East. It is a lay religious Order, by tradition military, chivalrous and nobiliary, which in time became sovereign on the islands of Rhodes and later of Malta.
Par. 2— In nations where it exercises its activity in virtue of its rights or of international conventions, the Order's structure comprises: Grand Priories, Priories, Subpriories and National Associations.
Par. 3—In this Constitution and in the Code the Sovereign Military Order of Malta is also referred to as "the Order of Malta" or simply as "the Order".
Par. 4 — In the rules which follow, the Grand Priories and the National Associations are also referred to as Priories and Associations. The term Code refers to the Code of the Order.

Article 2
Purpose
Par. 1 — The purpose of the Order is the promotion of the glory of God through the sanctification of its members, service to the faith and to the Holy Father, and assistance to one's neighbour, in accordance with its ancient traditions.
Par. 2 — True to the divine precepts and to the admonitions of our Lord Jesus Christ, guided by the teachings of the Church, the Order affirms and propagates the Christian virtues of charity and brotherhood. The Order carries out its charitable work for the sick, the needy and refugees without distinction of religion, race, origin and age.
The Order fulfils its institutional tasks especially by carrying out hospitaller works, including social and health assistance, as well as aiding victims of exceptional disasters and of war, attending also to their spiritual well-being and the strengthening of their faith in God.
Par. 3 — In order to be able to perform their institutional tasks, the Priories and Associations may, according to the regulations of the Code, establish dependent organizations in accordance with national laws and international conventions and agreements made with States.

Article 3
Sovereignty
Par. 1 — The Order is a subject of international law and exercises sovereign functions.
Par. 2 — Legislative, executive and judicial functions are reserved to the competent bodies of the Order according to the provisions of the Constitution and Code.

Article 4
Relations with the Apostolic See
Par. 1 — The Order is a legal entity recognized by the Holy See.
Par. 2— Religious members through their vows, as well as members of the Second Class through the Promise of Obedience, are only subject to their appropriate Superiors in the Order.
In accordance with the Code of Canon Law, the churches and conventual institutions of the Order are exempt from the jurisdiction of the dioceses and are directly subject to the Holy See.
Par. 3 — In the conduct of relations with the Apostolic See, the acquired rights, customs and privileges granted to the Order by the Supreme Pontiffs are in force unless expressly abrogated.
Par. 4 — The Supreme Pontiff appoints as his representative to the Order a Cardinal of the Holy Roman Church on whom are conferred the title of *Cardinalis Patronus* and special faculties. The *Cardinalis Patronus* has the task of promoting the spiritual interests of the Order and its members and relations between the Holy See and the Order.
Par. 5 — The Order has diplomatic representation to the Holy See, according to the norms of international law.
Par. 6 — The religious nature of the Order does not prejudice the exercise of sovereign prerogatives pertaining to the Order in so far as it is recognized by States as a subject of international law.

Article 5
Sources of the Order Law
The Sources of the Order's law are:
1 — the Constitution, the Code of the Order and, in addition, the provisions of Canon Law;
2 — the legislative provisions according to Art. 15, par. 2, a) of the Constitution;
3 — international agreements ratified according to Art. 15, par.2, h) of the Constitution;
4— the customs and privileges;
5 — the Code Rohan where not in contradiction to current norms.

Article 6
Flags, Insignia and Armorial Bearings of the Order
Par. 1 — The flag of the Order bears either the white Latin cross on a red field or the white eight— pointed cross (cross of Malta) on a red field.
Par. 2 — The armorial bearings of the Order display a white Latin cross on a red oval field, surrounded by a rosary, all superimposed on a white eight— pointed cross and displayed under a princely mantle surmounted by a crown.
Par. 3 — A special regulation, approved by the Grand Master with the deliberative vote of the Sovereign Council, defines the characteristics and the use of the flags, the insignia and the armorial bearings of the Order.

Article 7
Language
The official language of the Order is Italian.

Title II
THE MEMBERS OF THE ORDER

Article 8
The Classes
Par. 1 — The members of the Order are divided into three Classes:
A) the First Class consists of Knights of Justice, also called Professed, and of Professed Conventual Chaplains who have taken religious vows;
B) the Second Class consists of members in Obedience, who make the Promise according to Art. 9, par. 2, and who are subdivided into three ranks:
a) Knights and Dames of Honour and Devotion in Obedience
b) Knights and Dames of Grace and Devotion in Obedience
c) Magistral Knights and Dames in obedience
C) the Third Class consists of those members who do not make religious vows or the Promise but who live according to the norms of the Church and are prepared to commit themselves to the Order and the Church. They are divided, into six ranks:
a) Knights and Dames of Honour and Devotion
b) Conventual Chaplains *ad honorem*
c) Knights and Dames of Grace and Devotion
d) Magistral Chaplains
e) Knights and Dames of Magistral Grace
f) Donats (male and female) of Devotion
Par. 2 — The requisites for admission to the various classes and ranks of membership are determined by the Code.

Article 9

Obligations of the Members

Par. 1 — The Knights and Chaplains belonging to the First Class profess the vows of poverty, chastity and obedience in accordance with the Code, thus aspiring to perfection according to the Gospel. They are religious for all purposes of Canon Law and are governed by the particular rules which concern them. They are not obliged to live in community.

Par. 2— By virtue of the Promise, members of the Second Class oblige themselves to strive for the perfection of Christian life in conformity with the obligation of their state, in the spirit of the Order.

Par. 3 — The members of the Order are to conduct their lives in an exemplary manner in conformity with the teachings and precepts of the Church and to devote themselves to the charitable activities of the Order, according to the provisions of the Code.

Par. 4 — Members of the Second and of the Third Class, with the exception of priests, make a financial contribution through their national organizations to the Grand Magistry, fixed by the Chapter General.

Article 10

Assignment of Members

Par. 1 — Where only a Priory already exists, all members of the three Classes automatically belong to it.

Par. 2— Where a Subpriory is established, only the members of the First and Second Class belong to it.

Par. 3 — Where an Association is established, the members of the three Classes belong to it.

Par. 4—Where a Priory or Subpriory is established in the territory where already exists an Association, all the members of the First and Second Class are also members of the Priory or Subpriory.

Par. 5 — Where neither a Priory nor a Subpriory exists in the territory, the members of the First and Second Class not assigned to a Priory or Subpriory are directly incorporated in the Order *(in gremio religionis)*.

Par. 6— Where neither a Priory nor an Association exists in the territory, the members of the Third Class are assigned to an institution of the Order as the Grand Master decides.

Par. 7 — The Grand Master with the deliberative vote of the Sovereign Council, having heard the Priors, Regents or Presidents concerned, may transfer a member of the Order, with his consent, to a Priory, Subpriory or Association, according to the above norms.

Article 11
Duties and Offices
Par. 1 — The duties and offices of Grand Master and of Grand Commander are conferred upon Professed Knights in Perpetual Vows.
Par. 2 — The office of Prior is entrusted to Professed Knights in Perpetual or Temporary vows.
Par. 3 — The High Offices and the offices of the Sovereign Council, in keeping with Art. 20, par. 4, and the offices of Chancellor, Receiver and Hospitaller of the Priories and Subpriories as well as those of Regent, Lieutenant, Vicar and Procurator, are held preferably by Professed Knights. If Knights in Obedience are elected for their specific qualifications, their election must be confirmed by the Grand Master.
Par. 4 — The positions of High Officers, Priors, Vicars, Lieutenants, Procurators, Regents, Chancellors of Priories, and of at least four of the six Councillors of the Sovereign Council, are reserved to Knights having the requisites for Honour and Devotion or Grace and Devotion.

Title III
GOVERNMENT OF THE ORDER

Article 12
The Grand Master
Sovereign prerogatives and honours and the title "Most Eminent Highness" are reserved to the Grand Master, Head of the Order.

Article 13
Requisites for Election of Grand Master
Par. 1 — The Grand Master is elected for life by the Council Complete of State from among the Professed Knights with at least ten years in solemn vows if they are younger than fifty years of age; in the case of Professed Knights who are older, but who have been members of the Order for at least ten years, three years in solemn vows are sufficient.
Par. 2 — The Grand Master and the Lieutenant of the Grand Master must have the nobiliary requisites prescribed for the rank of Knights of Honour and Devotion.
Par. 3 — Before the assumption of the office, the election of the Grand Master is to be communicated by letter to the Holy Father by the person elected.

Article 14
The Grand Master's Oath
The person elected to the dignity of Grand Master, having informed the Holy Father of the election, takes the following oath in the presence of the *Cardinalis Patronus* in solemn session of the Council Complete of State:
"By this most Holy Wood of the Cross and by God's Holy Gospels, I, N. N., do solemnly promise and swear to observe the Constitution, the Code, the Rule and the laudable customs of our Order and to administer the affairs of the Order conscientiously. So help me God, and if I do otherwise, may it be to the risk of my soul."

Article 15
Powers of the Grand Master
Par. 1 — The Grand Master, assisted by the Sovereign Council, sees to the exercise of his supreme authority, to the conferral of duties and offices, and to the general government of the Order.
Par. 2 — It pertains to the Grand Master:
a) to issue legislative measures, with the deliberative vote of the Sovereign Council, concerning matters regulated neither by the Constitution nor by the Code;
b) to promulgate by decree the acts of government;
c) to admit, with the secret deliberative vote of the Sovereign Council, the members of the First Class to the Novitiate and to Temporary and Perpetual Vows as well as to admit members of the Second Class to the year of probation and to the Promise;
d) to admit, with the deliberative vote of the Sovereign Council, members of the First Class to Aspirancy;
e) to receive, with the deliberative vote of the Sovereign Council or with a provision *motu proprio,* members into the Third Class of the Order;
f) to administer, with the assistance of the Sovereign Council, the assets of the Common Treasure and to supervise the properties;
g) to execute the acts of the Holy See, insofar as these relate to the Order, and to inform the Holy See of the state and the needs of the Order;
h) to ratify international agreements, with the deliberative vote of the Sovereign Council
i) to convene an Extraordinary Chapter General which will have the faculty to dissolve the Sovereign Council and elect a new one, in accordance with the norms of the Constitution and Code.
Par. 3 — The decrees of par. 2 b) are designated magistral or conciliar depending on whether the act of government has been issued directly from the Grand Master or whether there has been prior consideration or prior deliberation by the Sovereign Council. When a deliberative vote is required, the Grand Master cannot issue a decree at variance with that vote, but he is not obliged to issue a decree in conformity with it.

Article 16
Resignation from Office by the Grand Master
The resignation from office by the Grand Master must be accepted by the Sovereign Council and, to be effective, communicated to the Holy Father.

Article 17
Extraordinary Government
Par. 1 — In the *case* of the permanent incapacity, resignation or death of the Grand Master, the Order is governed by a Lieutenant *ad interim* in the person of the Grand Commander who can carry out acts of ordinary administration until the Office ceases to be vacant.

Par. 2 —The permanent incapacity of the Grand Master is declared by the Magistral Court of first instance in closed session on a petition by a two thirds majority of the members of the Sovereign Council, which has been convened and chaired by the Grand Commander or the Grand Chancellor, or has convened itself by an absolute majority.

The petition is presented by the Grand Chancellor. or by a member of the Sovereign Council delegated for this purpose. If the petition is affirmed, the Grand Commander assumes the office of Lieutenant *ad interim*.

Par. 3 — In the case of the incapacity of the Grand Master for a period of more than one month, the Grand Commander assumes the ordinary administration of the Order and immediately convenes the Sovereign Council for confirmation.

Par. 4 — In the event of the incapacity of the Grand Commander, the Sovereign Council elects a Lieutenant *ad interim* in the person of one of its members, a Professed Knight in Perpetual Vows.

Par. 5 — The Lieutenant of the Grand Master is elected in accordance with Art. 23, par. 5, from among the Knights possessing the requisites required for election to Grand Master.

Before taking up his office, the Lieutenant of the Grand Master takes the oath in accordance with Art. 14.

The resignation of the Lieutenant of the Grand Master must be accepted by the Sovereign Council and, to be effective, the resolution must he communicated to the Holy Father.

Article 18
The High Offices
Par. 1 — The High Offices are :
the Grand Commander
the Grand Chancellor
the Grand Hospitaller
the Receiver of the Common Treasure .

Par. 2— The replacement of persons holding High Offices is regulated by the Code.

Article 19
The Prelate

Par. 1 — The Prelate is appointed by the Supreme Pontiff who chooses from among three candidates presented by the Grand Master with the deliberative vote of the Sovereign Council. In the event that none of the three candidates presented meets with the approval of the Holy Father, other candidates will be presented.

The Prelate assists the *Cardinalis Patronus* in carrying out his mission to the Order.

Par. 2 — The Prelate is the ecclesiastical superior of the clergy of the Order in sacerdotal functions. He ensures that the religious and priestly life of the Chaplains and their apostolate are conducted according to the discipline and the spirit of the order.

Par. 3 — The Prelate assists the Grand Master and the Grand Commander in their responsibility for both the life and religious observances of the members of the Order and in all matters concerning the spiritual nature of the works of the Order.

Par. 4— At each session of the Ordinary Chapter General the Prelate presents his report on the spiritual state of the Order.

Article 20
The Sovereign Council

Par. 1 — The Sovereign Council assists the Grand Master in the Government of the Order.

Par. 2 — The following are members of Sovereign Council:
a) the Grand Master or the Lieutenant, who presides;
b) the holders of the four High Offices and six Councillors.

Par. 3 — The members of the Sovereign Council, excluding the Grand Master and the Lieutenant, are elected by the Chapter General by a majority of those present .

Par. 4 — The Grand Commander and at least four other members of the Sovereign Council must be Professed Knights in Perpetual or Temporary Vows .

Par. 5 — For the admission of members to the First Class only the members of the Sovereign Council who are Professed Knights in Perpetual or Temporary Vows are entitled to vote.

Par. 6 — The members of the Sovereign Council remain in office until the next Chapter General and may be re-elected. For a third or further consecutive re-election to the same position a two-thirds majority of votes of those present is required .

Par. 7 — The Grand Master does not vote on matters for which the Sovereign Council has a deliberative vote or must give its advice, notwithstanding Art. 15, par. 3.

In the case of a tie vote among the Councillors, including the High Officers, the decision of the Grand Master prevails. If the Grand Master does not express an opinion, the matter is suspended.

Article 21
The Government Council
Par. 1 — The Government Council is a consultative body for the discussion of the political, religious, hospitaller and international policies of the Order or other general aspects of the life of the Order. It may issue recommendations to the holders of the four High Offices and to the Board of Auditors. It meets at least twice each year.
Par. 2 — The Government Council consists of six Councillors from different geographic areas elected by the Chapter General from members of any of the three Classes of the Order.
Par. 3 — At meetings of the Government Council are present:
a) the Grand Master or the Lieutenant, who convenes it and presides
b) the members of the Sovereign Council;
c) the Prelate of the Order, when there might be questions within his competence.
Par. 4 — The six Councillors remain in office until the next Chapter General and may he re-elected once.

Article 22
The Chapter General
Par. 1 — The Chapter General is the supreme assembly of the Order and is composed of representatives of the different classes. It is convened once every five years or whenever the Grand Master, having heard the Sovereign Council, may think fit, or on application to the Grand Master by the majority of the Priories, Sub- priories and Associations.
Par. 2 — The following are members of the Chapter General:
a) the Grand Master ot the Lieutenant, who presides;
b) the members of the Sovereign Council;
c) the Prelate;
d) the Priors, or in the event of vacancy , their permanent substitutes (Procurators, Vicars, Lieutenants);
e) the Professed Bailiffs;
f) two Professed Knights, and in the absence of one of these a Knight in Obedience, delegated by each Priory;
g) a Professed Knight and a Knight in Obedience delegated by the Knights *in gremio religionis;*
h) five Regents of the Subpriories;
i) fifteen representatives of the Associations, in accordance with the Code;
j) the six members of the Government Council of the Order.
Par. 3 — The Chapter General is convened to elect the members of the Sovereign Council, the members of the Government Council, the members of the Board of Auditors; to deal with modifications to the Constitution and the Code; to take cognizance of and deal with the most important problems pertaining to the Order, such as

its spiritual and temporal state, the programme of its activities and its international relations.

Par. 4 — For the approval of modifications to the Constitution, a majority of two-thirds is required. For the approval of modifications to the Code, an absolute majority is required, with the exception of Arts. 6—93, which refer exclusively to the First Class, for which it is required that in the absolute majority vote there is also the majority of the Professed Knights having the right to vote.

Article 23
The Council Complete of State

Par. 1 — The Council Complete of State elects the Grand Master or the Lieutenant of the Grand Master.

Par. 2 — The following are entitled to vote:

a) the Lieutenant of the Grand Master or the Lieutenant *ad interim;*

b) the members of the Sovereign Council;

c) the Prelate;

d) the Priors or, in the event of vacancy, their permanent substitutes (Procurators, Vicars, Lieutenants);

e) the Professed Bailiffs;

f) two Professed Knights delegated by each Priory;

g) a Professed Knight and a Knight in Obedience delegated by the Knights *in gremio religionis;*

h) five Regents of the Suhpriories;

i) fifteen representatives of the Associations, in accordance with the Code.

Par. 3 — The Grand Master's election requires the majority plus one of those present entitled to vote.

Par. 4 — The members of the First Class taking part in the Council Complete of State have the right to propose three candidates. In the event that such a list is not presented within the first day of the meetings of the Council Complete of State or if a candidate is not elected from among the proposed list within the first three ballots, the members of the Council Complete of State have freedom of choice in successive ballots.

Par. 5 — After the fifth undecided ballot, the Council Complete of State decides, with the same majority, whether to proceed to the election of a Lieutenant of the Grand Master, for a maximum period of one year. In the event of a negative result the balloting to elect the Grand Master resumes. In the event of a positive result the Lieutenant of the Grand Master is elected by means of a runoff ballot between the two candidates who received the largest number of votes in the fifth ballot. The candidate in the runoff ballot who receives the larger number of votes prevails. Should there be only one candidate, a majority vote of those present is required.

Par. 6 — If elected, the Lieutenant of the Grand Master must convene the Council Complete of State before the end of his mandate.

Article 24
General Norms for Elections
Par. 1 — The members of the Chapter General , of the Council Complete of State, and those entitled to vote in the election of a Prior, Regent or President of an Association, must act personally and may not appoint any representatives, or delegates or proxies or vote by letter, except as provided in Art. 196 of the Code.
Par. 2 — Without prejudice to any other provision, the basis of any vote is calculated on those with a right to vote who are present and vote. Where applicable, a two-thirds majority applies only for the first three ballots. For successive ballots a majority of those present having the right to vote is sufficient, without prejudice to any other provision.

Article 25
The Juridical Council
Par. 1 — The Juridical Council is an expert advisory collegial body, which can be consulted about juridical questions and problems of special importance.
Par. 2 — It is composed of a President, a Vice-President, a Secretary General and four members.
Par. 3 — The members are appointed by the Grand Master with the advice of the Sovereign Council. They are selected from among those who are experts in the juridical sciences, preferably members of the Order particularly versed in the law of the Order, in public and international law and in Canon Law. They remain in office for three years and may be re-appointed.

Article 26
Judicial Regulations
Par. 1 — Cases falling within the jurisdiction of the ecclesiastical forum are submitted to the ordinary ecclesiastical Tribunals, in accordance with Canon Law.
Par. 2 — For cases falling within the competence of the lay forum between physical and juridical persons of the Order and against third parties, the juridical function is exercised by the Magistral Courts, in accordance with the Code.
Par. 3 — The Grand Master, with the deliberative vote of the Sovereign Council, appoints the Presidents, the judges, and the clerk of the Magistral Courts.
Par. 4 — The judges of the Magistral Courts are chosen from among members of the Order who are specially versed in law. They hold office for three years an may be re-appointed.
Par. 5 — The judicial regulations and the procedure to be observed by the Magistral courts are regulated by the Code.

Article 27

The Board of Auditors

Par. 1 — The Board of Auditors oversees and controls the income, the expenditure and all the assets of the Order. It is also the consultative body of the Receiver of the Common Treasure.

Par. 2 — It consists of a President, four ordinary Councillors, and two alternates.

Par. 3 — The members of the Board of Auditors are elected by the Chapter General in the first balloting, with a majority of those having the right to vote and with the same majority in successive ballots. They are chosen from among the Knights versed in the juridical, economic and financial disciplines. They hold office until the following Chapter General, and may he re-elected for one consecutive term and, with a two-thirds majority, for a third term.

Title IV
THE ORGANIZATION OF THE ORDER

Article 28

Establishment of Organizations

Par. 1 — The establishment of a Grand Priory, Priory, Subpriory or Association, and the approval of their statutes, belongs to the Grand Mister with the deliberative vote of the Sovereign Council,

Par. 2 — The title of Grand Priory belongs to some Priories by custom or by virtue of a resolution of the Chapter General.

Par. 3 — The Grand Master, with the advice of the competent Priories, Subpriories or Associations and the deliberative vote of the Sovereign Council, establishes new organizations and approves their statutes. The establishment of Priories and Subpriories is to be communicated to the Holy Father.

Par. 4 — The same procedure must be followed for the amalgamation, division or dissolution of Priories, Subpriories or Associations.

Par. 5 — Within each territory, only a Priory or a Subpriory can be established. Relations between a Priory and an Association existing in the same territory are regulated by the Code.

Article 29

Government of Priories

Par. 1 — At least five Professed Knights are necessary for the establishment of a Priory.

Par. 2 — The members of the three Classes belong to the Assembly.

Par. 3 — The Prior is assisted by a limited Council, called the Chapter, elected according to the, statutes of the Priory.

Par. 4 — The following are members of the Chapter:

a) the Prior;

b) the Professed Knights and Chaplains of the Priory;

c) the Chancellor, the Receiver and, where no Association exists in the same territory, the Hospitaller;

d) two representatives of the Second Class;

e) two representatives of the Third Class, where no Association exists.

Par. 5 — The Chancellor and the Receiver are appointed by the Prior from among the Knights of the First and Second Class, having consulted the members of the First Class.

The Hospitaller and the representatives of the Second and Third Class are elected by the Assembly.

Par. 6 — The Professed members propose by a majority vote a list of three candidates from which the members of the Priory Chapter elect the Prior.

Par. 7 — The Prior elect may not take up office. until he has received the approval of the Grand Master, with the deliberative vote of the Sovereign Council, and taken the oath.

Par. 8 — The statutes of the Priory establish the other competencies of the Chapter and of the Assembly.

Article 30
Term of Office of Priors

The Prior and the members of the limited Council remain in office for six years and may be re-elected. Re-election to a third or further six-year term requires a two-thirds majority.

Article 31
Lieutenant of the Prior

Par. 1 — Whenever expediency and need require, the Prior, after hearing the Chapter, may appoint a Lieutenant to substitute for him for one year, in all or in part, in the exercise of his duties. The appointment is to be approved by the Grand Master, with the advice of the Sovereign Council.

Par. 2 — In case of necessity, the appointment of the Lieutenant devolves on the Grand Master with the advice of the Sovereign Council, if the Prior has not made provision in accordance with par. 1.

Par. 3 — The Prior, after hearing the limited Council, can appoint a Lieutenant to substitute for him for a maximum period of three months.

Par. 4 — The Lieutenant must be a Professed Knight or a Knight in Obedience, in accordance with Art. 11, par. 3.

Article 32
Vicar and Procurator of a Priory
Par. 1 — For just and grave cause the Grand Master may, with the deliberative vote of the Sovereign Council, remove a Prior and appoint a Vicar.
Par. 2 — Should it not be possible to proceed with the election of a Prior in accordance with Canon Law, the Vicar remains in office until the end of the next Chapter General.
Par. 3 — Should a Prior be prevented from fulfilling his tasks, or for other just and grave reasons, the Grand Master, with the deliberative vote of the Sovereign Council, is to appoint a Procurator who shall remain in office until the end of the next Chapter General.
Par. 4 — The Vicar and the Procurator must be Professed Knights or Knights in Obedience in accordance with Art. 11 par. 3.

Article 33
Subpriories and the Appointment of Regents
Par. 1 — For the establishment of a Subpriory there must be at least nine Knights in Obedience.
Par. 2 — The Subpriory is governed by a Professed Knight or a Knight in Obedience, with the title of Regent, assisted by a Council and the Chapter, in accordance with its own Statutes and the Code.
Par. 3 — The Regent and the Councillors are elected by the Chapter. The Regent takes office after having received the approval of the Grand Master, with the deliberative vote of the Sovereign Council, and having taken the oath.
Par. 4 —The Regent and the Councillors hold office for six years and may be re-elected. For a third and successive reelection a two-thirds majority is required.

Article 34
Associations
Par. 1 — Associations are established by decree of the Grand Master, with the deliberative vote of the Sovereign Council. Their statutes are drafted in accordance with the legislation of the countries in which they are established and are approved by the Grand Master, with the deliberative vote of the Sovereign Council.
Par. 2 — The Grand Master, with the advice of the Sovereign Council, confirms the appointment of the President and the members of the Board of Directors. The term of office is determined by the statutes and lasts from a minimum of three to a maximum of six years. If provided in the statutes, re-election is possible.

Article 35

Delegations

Par. 1 — The Priories. the Subpriories and the Associations may form regional Delegations in accordance with the Code.

Par. 2 — The Delegations are composed of all members of the Priories, Subpriories and Associations who reside in the territory. Their rules are established in conformity with the statutes of the respective Priories, Subpriories and Associations and a regulation approved by the Grand Master, with the deliberative vote of the Sovereign Council.

Par. 3 — The Delegation is directed by a member of the Order who has the title of Delegate and who is appointed in the first instance by his own Superior with the advice of the respective Council, and subsequently elected by the members of the Delegation and confirmed by the Superior. The Delegation of a Priory or Subpriory, where possible, should be entrusted to a Professed Knight or a Knight in Obedience.

Par. 4 — The Delegate is assisted by a Council consisting of not more than five members and a Chaplain, who has under his care the spiritual life of the members of the Delegation.

Article 36

Text and Official Translations of the Constitution

Par. 1 — The text of the Constitution is written in the Italian language. The Grand Master with the advice of the Sovereign Council shall provide for the official translation in English, French, German and Spanish.

Par. 2 — The text in Italian, bearing the signature of the Head of the Order and the Seal of State, is kept in the Archives of the Grand Magistery.

Par. 3 — In cases of different interpretations, the official Italian text prevails.

Article 37

Transitional Regulations

The Grand Master, with the deliberative vote of the Sovereign Council, issues transitional norms to regulate matters pending when the Constitution and Code come into effect.

signed / Carlo Marullo di Condojanni
Grand Chancellor

signed Fra' Andrew Bertie

CODE
OF THE SOVEREIGN MILITARY
HOSPITALLER ORDER
OF ST. JOHN OF JERUSALEM
OF RHODES AND OF MALTA

promulgated 1 August 1966
reformed by the Extraordinary Chapter General of
28-30 April 1997

INDEX

Title I
GENERAL REGULATIONS

Article 1
Nature of the Code of the Order of Malta
This Code regulates the life, the organization and the activity of the Order.

Article 2
Interpretation of Laws
Par. 1 — Authentic interpretation belongs to those who issue the laws.
Par. 2 — The interpretation of the laws is the exclusive competency of the Magistral Courts and, in a non-binding way, of the Juridical Council.

Article 3
Publication and Promulgation of Laws
The laws and official decrees are published in the *Bolletino Officiale* and, unless otherwise determined, they become effective one month after date of publication.

Article 4
Dispensation from Laws
The Grand Master, within the limits of the Constitution, may dispense in individual cases from the observance of the provisions of this Code, except in matters of vows, the prescriptions of ecclesiastical law and the structure of the Government.

Article 5
The Name of the Order
The name of the Order, according to Art. 1, par. 3 of the Constitution, may be abbreviated to SMOM or another designation, according to the respective languages. Other designations will have to be approved by the Sovereign Council.

Title II
THE MEMBERS OF THE FIRST CLASS

CHAPTER I
Members of the First Class
First Section
Admission

Article 6
Requirements for Admission to the First Class
Any Catholic may be admitted to the First Class of the Order who:
a) is not subject to any impediment established by the Constitution, the Code or Canon Law;
b) is moved by right intention;
c) is suited to serve the sick and the poor of Jesus Christ and to dedicate himself to the service of the Church and of the Holy See according to the spirit of the Order;
d) meets other requirements prescribed by the Priories or Subpriories.

Article 7
Request for Admission
Par. 1 — A candidate for Professed Knight must address his request for admission to the competent territorial Priory or Subpriory.
Par. 2 — If a Priory or Subpriory does not exist in the region where the candidate resides, the request for admission is to be presented directly to the Grand Magstery of the Order.

Article 8
Verification of Requirements for Admission
Par. 1 — The Prior or the Regent or the Grand Magistery is to request advice concerning the application of the candidate from the President of his Association, where one exists.
Par. 2 — Before seeking the advice mentioned above, and being assured that the necessary requirements have been fulfilled, the Prior or Regent, with the deliberative vote of his Chapter, is to ask the Grand Master for the *nihil obstat* for admission to Aspirancy, which is granted by the Grand Master, with the deliberative vote of the Sovereign Council.

Article 9

Requirements for the Admissibility of the Request

Par. 1 — No one may be validly admitted to the Novitiate who:

a) is not a member of the Order for at least one year;

b) has not completed 22 years of age;

c) is under investigation by the courts.

Par. 2 — In addition, the norms of can. 643 § 1 nn. 2-5 of the Code of Canon Law also apply.

Article 10

Requirements for Licit Admission to the Novitiate

For admission to the Novitiate it is required that the aspirant:

a) shall not have presented his request under force, grave fear or fraud;

b) shall not be encumbered by debts which he is unable to meet;

c) is not involved in matters which could involve the Order in any type of controversy;

d) shall, at the time of his admission, be exempt from legal or moral obligations towards ancestors or descendants.

e) has not abandoned the Catholic Church or adhered to another religion;

f) has not been suspended from the practice of his profession,

g) has not been convicted of a crime either civil or ecclesiastical or activity under civil or ecclesiastical prosecution;

h) does not belong to an organization with an objective contrary to the spirit and norms of the Catholic Church.

Article 11

Dispensation from Impediments for the Admission to the Novitiate

Par. 1 — Dispensation from impediments imposed by the canon Law is reserved the Holy See.

Par. 2 — Dispensation from other impediments is granted by the Grand Master, with the consent of the Sovereign Council.

Article 12

Documents Required for Admission

For admission to the Novitiate the following are required:

a) certificates of baptism and confirmation;

b) certificate confirming unmarried or free status;

c) testimonial letters from the respective Ordinaries of the places where the aspirants after eighteen years of age have resided for more than five years;

d) testimonial letters from the respective Superiors for those aspirants who have belonged to a seminary, college or novitiate of another institute of consecrated life or society of apostolic life;

e) favourable testimonial letters from the Superior of the organization within the territory in which the aspirant resides or, in its absence, from the Prior or Regent of the Priory to which the aspirant is to be aggregated;

f) such other testimonials as the competent Superiors may consider useful.

Article 13
Testimonial Letters
Those from whom the testimonial letters referred to in Art. 12 are requested. must send them to the competent Superior within three months of the request. They should be sealed and, except for Bishops, given under oath. Anyone who for serious reasons considers that he cannot reply, should report on the matter to the Grand Master within the prescribed period of three months.

Article 14
Supplementary Information
If the person from whom information is sought does not know the aspirant sufficiently well, the Superiors of the Order should obtain additional accurate and reliable information. If the information is not sufficiently complete, the matter must be referred to the Grand Master.

Article 15
Purpose of Testimonial Letters
Testimonial letters should contain information, after diligent and conscientious research, concerning the birth, habits, character, reputation, social condition and educational level of the Aspirant and whether the conditions of Arts. 9 and 10 are met.

Article 16
Secrecy Regarding information
Anyone who learns of the content of the testimonial letters or of information obtained, is bound to secrecy regarding that information and the persons who have furnished it.

Second Section
Aspirancy and Novitiate

Article 17
Those Responsible for Aspirants
Par. 1 — Once the application for admission has been accepted, the Aspirant is entrusted by the Superior to an expressly delegated Professed Knight, or to a Spiritual Father, for a period of orientation and formation about the Order.
Par. 2 — The delegated Knight or Spiritual Father must make a written report to the Superior on the personality, conduct and suitability of the Aspirant.

Article 18
Duration of Aspirancy
Aspirancy must last a minimum of three months and a maximum of one year, during which time the Aspirant must present a written request to be admitted to the Novitiate.

Article 19
Establishment and Validity of the Novitiate
Par. 1 — The Priories or Subpriories of the Order may establish a Novitiate, with a decree of the Grand Master and the advice of the Sovereign Council.
Par. 2— On admission to the Novitiate, the Grand Master with the advice of the Professed members of the Sovereign Council, may, for important reasons connected with the personal circumstances of the candidate, provide that he spend the period of his Novitiate in the place of his previous domicile. This may be done provided that it is always guaranteed the candidate have frequent contact with the Novice Master; that the theoretical and practical formation of the Novice in both charisms of the Order – the protection of the faith and the service of the poor (*tuitio fidei et obsequium pauperum*) – is assured; and that instruction from an assistant selected from the First or Second Class in accordance with the norms of Art. 20, Par. 2 may be imparted on the historical development of the Order, its traditions, and its juridical evolution.

Article 20
Novice Master
Par. 1 — The Grand Master chooses the Novice Master and his assistant. The Novice Master must be chosen from among priests and, if possible, from the Conventual Chaplains, while the assistant should be selected, if possible, from the Professed Knights and have completed his 35th year of age. The Novice Master is responsible for the formation and spiritual instruction of the Novice.

Par. 2 — Whenever a Professed Knight distinguished for wisdom and a profound knowledge of the history and juridical situation of the Order is not available in the immediate vicinity of the Novice, the Grand Master, with the consent of the Professed members of the Sovereign Council, is to choose the assistant from the Knights in Obedience.

Article 21
Admission of Aspirants to the Novitiate
Par. 1 — It pertains to the Grand Master, with the consent of the competent Chapter and the Professed members of the Sovereign Council, to admit Aspirants to the Novitiate.
Par. 2 — Knights belonging to the Second Class can ask for direct admission to the Novitiate without passing through the status of Aspirant, subject to Arts. 9 and 10.

Article 22
Spiritual Exercises prior to the Novitiate
The Aspirant, before beginning the Novitiate, is obliged to complete a course of spiritual exercise of eight full days in an approved place, beginning with a general confession, if that is the prudent judgement of the confessor.

Article 23
Entry into the Novitiate
The Novitiate begins in accordance with the norms set forth in the Ceremonial and it is to be recorded in a certified document.

Article 24
Duration of the Novitiate
Par. 1 — The Novitiate must last one uninterrupted year.
Par. 2 — The Novitiate may not be extended beyond two years.

Article 25
Change of Residence of the Novice
Par. 1 — Any change of residence of the Novice during the Novitiate must be authorized by the Superior having consulted the Novice Master.
Par. 2 — In case it is necessary for the Novice to change residence, he may be transferred to the care of a Novice Master who resides in the place to which the candidate moves.

Article 26
Change of Location of the Novitiate
On request of the Novice, a Novitiate begun in one prioral or sub-prioral territory may be continued in another. The transfer must be approved by the Grand Master, having consulted the competent Superiors.

Article 27
Promulgation of the Regulations of the Novitiate
The regulations for the formation of Novices are promulgated by the Grand Master, with the consent of the Professed members of the Sovereign Council.

Article 28
Duties of Novices
The Novice under the direction of the Novice Master should apply himself to pious exercises and to his religious formation as the regulations provide. He must also study the Rule, the laws and the history of the Order.
The Novice should also be active in works of mercy and, where possible, in the Order's works to which he is called by virtue of the religious vows he seeks to profess.

Article 29
Duties of the Novice Master
The Novice Master is to take care that the Novice is faithful to the religious observances as prescribed for Professed Knights.

Article 30
Semi-annual Report of the Novice Master to the Superiors
Every six months the Novice Master is to provide a written report to the competent Superior, who, with his Council, shall arrange to inform the Grand Master.

Article 31
Request for Admission to Profession
Shortly before the conclusion of the probationary period, the Novice who intends to make vows is to present, through his Superior, a written request to the Grand Master for admission to profession of temporary vows.

Article 32
Spiritual Exercises in Preparation for Profession
In preparation for the profession of temporary vows, the Novice is to undertake a course of spiritual exercises of eight hill days in an approved place.

Third Section
Professed Knights in Temporary Vows

Article 33
Admission to Profession
After presentation by the competent Superior, who must have the consent of his Chapter, it pertains to the Grand Master, with the consent of the Professed members of the Sovereign Council and having heard the opinion of the Prelate of the Order, to admit Knights to first profession of temporary vows.

Article 34
Requirements for the Validity of Profession
For the validity of profession it is required that:
a) it be preceded by the Novitiate as prescribed by Art. 23 and following;
b) it be received by the Grand Master, or by the competent Superior, or by one delegated by them;
c) it be expressed and freely made.

Article 35
Renewal of Temporary Vows
Par. 1 — When each period for which the vows were taken has elapsed, the Professed Knight at his request will be permitted by his Superior to renew them.
Par. 2 — During the first three years, temporary vows must be renewed each year immediately after they expire. In the following three-year periods, they will be renewed at the end of each *triennium*. The period of temporary vows must not exceed nine years.
Par. 3 — The competent Superior, for just cause, can permit the renewal of temporary vows to be anticipated by one month, always provided that the full period preceding perpetual profession has elapsed.

Article 36
Spiritual Retreat for the Renewal of Vows
The renewal of vows must be preceded by a spiritual retreat of three days.

Article 37
Formula of Religious Profession
The Novice Knight, in accordance with the Ceremonial of the Order, is to pronounce the following formula before the competent Superior, or one delegated by him, in the presence of two witnesses:

"I, NN, vow to Almighty God, imploring the assistance of His Immaculate Mother, of Saint John the Baptist and of Blessed Gerard, to observe poverty, chastity, and obedience for one year (three years; in perpetuity) to whichever Superior I will be assigned by the Holy Order and I intend to make these vows in the spirit of the statutes and laws of the Order of Malta".

Article 38
Custody of the Document of Religious Profession
The document containing the formula of religious profession, testifying to the profession and to its renewals signed by the Knight, by the one who received them and by the witnesses, must be kept in the archives of the Grand Magistery, and a certified copy must be kept in the archives of the respective Priory, Subpriory, or Association.

Article 39
The Ability to Leave Religious Profession on the Expiry of Vows
At the expiry of temporary vows, a Knight is free to leave religious profession and to return to his previous Class.

Article 40
Appointment of the Spiritual Director for the Professed in Temporary Vows
The Grand Master, with the advice of the Professed members of the Sovereign Council and the competent Prior, appoints the Spiritual Director of the Professed in Temporary Vows choosing him from among the Conventual Chaplains, Conventual Chaplains *ad honorem* or Magistral Chaplains, provided there are no grave reasons to the contrary.

Article 41
Duties of Knights in Temporary Vows
Par. 1 — Knights in Temporary Vows are bound to the pious exercises and specialization courses prescribed by the respective regulations.
Par. 2 — Under the guidance of the Spiritual Director, and in accordance with the existing regulations of the various institutions and works of the Order, the Knight in Temporary Vows must dedicate himself to works of mercy "as a servant of our Lords the poor and the sick" and to the defence of the Catholic faith.

Article 42
Report by the Spiritual Director to the Superiors of the Professed in Temporary Vows
At least every year. the Spiritual Director must inlbrm the competent Superiors regarding the religious life of the Knight in Temporary Vows and his activity in the works of the Order.

Article 43
Rights and Privileges of Professed in Temporary Vows
Par. 1 — Professed Knights in Temporary Vows enjoy the same privileges and spiritual favours to which the Professed in Perpetual Vows have a right. On their death, they have the right to the same prayers.
Par. 2 — Professed Knights in Temporary Vows have an active and passive voice unless otherwise provided in the Constitution and in the Code.

Article 44
Effects of the Profession of Temporary Vows
The profession of temporary vows renders acts contrary to them unlawful but not invalid.

Fourth Section
Professed Knights in Perpetual Vows

Article 45
Requirements for the Validity of Perpetual Profession
For the validity of perpetual profession it is required:
a) that the Knight have completed 30 years of age;
b) that he make the profession immediately after the end of the period of temporary vows;
c) that the Knight be admitted to Profession by the Grand Master with the advice of the Sovereign Council, upon presentation by the competent Superior and Chapter;
d) that the *nihil obstat* of the Prelate of the Order be obtained;
e) that the Profession be made freely, according to the norms of Canon Law;
f) that it be received by the Grand Master, or by one delegated by him, or the competent Superior, provided he is a Professed Knight.

Article 46
Duration Of Temporary Vows required for Perpetual Profession
Par. 1 — For the validity of perpetual profession, in addition to the provisions of Art. 45, it is required that the period of temporary profession be at least five continuous years, whenever the aspirant has not completed forty years of age.
Par. 2 — For Knights over forty years of age, three years of temporary profession are sufficient, provided the conditions prescribed in Arts. 34 and 45 have been observed.

Article 47

Spiritual Exercises in Preparation for Perpetual Profession

Perpetual profession must be preceded by a course of spiritual exercises of eight days in an approved place.

Article 48

Perpetual Profession

Par. 1 — Perpetual profession must be made in accordance with the Ceremonial of the Order.

Par. 2 — The document containing the formula of religious profession, testifying to the profession of perpetual vows, must be signed by the Knight who has made the vows, by the person who received the profession, and by two witnesses. A certified copy is to be kept in the archives of the Grand Magistery and also in the archives of the respective Priory or Subpriory or Association.

Par. 3 — The Superior must inform the parish priest of the place of baptism of the Professed Knight in Perpetual Vows in order that an entry of the fact may be made in the baptismal register.

Article 49

Effects of Perpetual Profession

Perpetual profession renders acts contrary to it not only unlawful but also invalid, provided that the law of the Church so prescribes.

Fifth Section
Professed Conventual Chaplains

Article 50

Duties of Conventual Chaplains

Professed Conventual Chaplains with religious vows consecrate themselves to God and, under the authority of the Superiors, dedicate themselves to the pastoral care of the members of the Order, to religious assistance towards its charitable and missionary works, and to the service of its churches.

Article 51

Provisions of the Code concerning Conventual Chaplains

What the Code establishes regarding admission to the Order, the Novitiate and the profession of Knights is applicable to Professed Conventual Chaplains, without prejudice to particular dispositions of Canon Law and Arts. 52 and following.

Article 52
Requirements for Admission of Conventual Chaplains
Par. 1 — Clerics who have received ordination to the priesthood may be admitted to profession as Conventual Chaplains of the Order.
Par. 2 — Those who intend to be ordained priests may be accepted as Aspirants to the Novitiate for Conventual Chaplains, and once they have been ordained deacon, may be admitted to the Novitiate.
The Grand Master, with the advice of the Sovereign Council and the approval of the Prelate, issues special rules for Aspirancy.
Par. 3 — Before admission to Aspirancy or the Novitiate, approval of the Prelate and of the Ordinary is required.

Article 53
Master of Conventual Chqplains in the Novitiate
Par. 1 — The Master of Conventual Chaplains in the Novitiate must be a priest, proposed by the Prelate of the Order, who is either himself a Professed of the Order, or failing this, of another religious Institute.
Par. 2 — Every six months, the Master of Chaplains in the Novitiate must present a report to the competent Superiors through the Prelate on the suitability and conduct of each Novice.

Article 54
Duration of the Novitiate for Conventual Chaplains
The Novitiate for Conventual Chaplains is to be completed according to the norms of Canon Law and in conformity with Art. 19, par. 2, and must last for at least one year.

Article 55
Temporary Profession of Conventual Chaplains
At the conclusion of the Novitiate, the Conventual Chaplain makes profession of temporary vows for a three year period, in accordance with Canon Law.

Article 56
Formula for Temporary Profession of Conventual Chaplains
In making profession, the Conventual Chaplain pronounces the formula according to the Ceremonial with the same requirements as set forth in Art. 37.

Article 57
Perpetual Profession of Conventual Chaplains
At the end of the period of temporary vows, the Conventual Chaplain makes profession of perpetual vows in accordance with the prescriptions of Canon Law.

Article 58

Ecclesiastical Discipline for Conventual Chaplains

Par. 1 — Professed Conventual Chaplains are directly subject to the Prelate of the Order in matters relating to ecclesiastical discipline. The Prelate is assisted by Chaplains having the title of Prefect.

Par. 2 — The Grand Master, with the consent of the Sovereign Council and the like opinion of the Prelate, may issue a special regulation for Conventual Chaplains.

Article 59

Rights of and Norms for Professed Conventual Chaplains

Par. 1 — Professed Conventual Chaplains in Perpetual Vows have a voice in Prioral or subprioral Chapters.

Par. 2 — Professed Conventual Chaplains must observe the Ceremonial regarding the use of the habit.

Article 60

The Canonical Title of Poverty of Professed Conventual Chaplains

With profession, Conventual Chaplains acquire the canonical title of poverty. Where necessary, the Order assures them of an adequate means of support in accordance with Canon Law.

CHAPTER II
Religious Vows

First Section
The Vow of Obedience

Article 61

The Virtue of Obedience

The virtue of obedience moves the soul to the imitation of Jesus Christ who became obedient even unto death on the Cross.

Article 62

The Vow of Obedience

With the vow of obedience, Professed Knights and Chaplains bind themselves to obey the Holy Father and their legitimate Superiors in accordance with the Constitution and Code.

Article 63
The Precept of the Vow of Obedience
Par. 1 — Superiors convey orders by virtue of the vow when they use the formula "in virtue. .", or "in the name of God..." or some analogous form.
Par. 2 — The command cannot be imposed except for serious and just cause and must be given in writing or in the presence of two witnesses.

Article 64
Observance of the Laws of the Order
The prescriptions contained in the laws of the Order of themselves do not contain a precept under pain of sin unless they concern a matter relating to the vows, or to divine law.

Article 65
Relations with Superiors of the Order
The Professed must have the required religious respect for their Superiors, and must submit themselves to them in a spirit of love and devotion. Such respect does not conflict with the liberty to make known to such Superiors whatsoever they may think useful for the benefit of the Order.

Article 66
Spirit of Collaboration between Members and Superiors
In order to promote unity and harmony, the Professed must maintain fraternal relations and confer regularly with their Superiors and be assiduous in attendance at meetings.

Second Section
The Vow of Chastity

Article 67
The Vow of Chastity
Par. 1 — The vow of chastity binds the Professed, also by the virtue of religion, to live celibately and to avoid every internal or external act contrary to Christian purity.
Par. 2 — The temporary vow of chastity constitutes an impedient impediment and the perpetual vow of chastity constitutes a diriment impediment to marriage.

Article 68
Spiritual Aids for the Practice of Chastity
Par. 1 — In order to remain faithful to his vow of chastity, the Professed should make use of spiritual aids such as, principally, the frequent reception of the sacraments of penance and the Eucharist, a filial devotion to the Immaculate Virgin, mortification of the senses, and profound humility.
Par. 2 — The Professed, not being bound to the common life, should be even more careful to avoid being involved in worldly social gatherings and entertainments. He must seek to give edification through his conduct, honouring his state as a religious in the Order of Malta.

Third Section
The Vow of Poverty

Article 69
The Vow of Poverty
By the temporary vow of poverty, the Professed renounces the independent use of temporal goods, in accordance with norms of this Code.

Article 70
Effects of the Temporary Vow of Poverty
The Professed in Temporary Vows retain the ownership of their goods and the capacity, even through inheritance, to acquire other goods.

Article 71
Prohibition against Donations
The Professed in Temporary Vows cannot make gifts of their goods *inter vivos*.

Article 72
The Will prior to Profession
Par. 1 — Before profession, the Novice must make a Will disposing freely of his present and future goods. After profession, the Will cannot be changed without the permission of the competent Superior of the Order.
Par. 2 — The original Will or a copy, under sealed cover, is to be submitted to the Superior of the Order, who must see that it is properly kept.
Par. 3 — The candidate for profession must give an inventory of his estate to the Superior, who is to ensure that it is sealed and kept confidential.

Article 73
Rights of the Order over the Goods of the Professed
Everything which the Professed acquires through his activity or by reason of his membership in the Order *(intuitu religionis)* devolves to the Order.

Article 74
Goods acquired "intuitu religionis"
In the absence of a specific declaration to the contraiy, it is assumed that any gift or legacy to the Professed is intended to he *intuitu religionis.*

Article 75
Use and Usufruct of Personal Goods
Par. 1 — In accordance with the Code of Canon Law, before temporary vows and for their duration, the Novice must cede to a person of his choice the administration of his goods and arrange for their use or enjoyment.
The Novice, after making temporary vows, must keep a part of the income from his property to maintain his standard of living and to support the works of the Order.
Par. 2 — With the consent of the Grand Master, and the deliberative vote of the majority of the Professed Knights of the Sovereign Council, the Professed Knight may retain the administration of his goods even after making temporary vows, mindful of what is set out in par. I.
Within the limits foreseen in this Code, he must always administer his goods, as regards their use and enjoyment, with the care and diligence of a good head of household.

Article 76
Conditions regarding the Use of the Privilege for Administration, Use and Usufruct of Goods
With the permission of the Grand Master, in accordance with Art. 75 and always under the direction of the Grand Prior or Prior, the Professed is to provide for:
a) ordinary personal expenses, such as food, lodging, and clothing in accord with his social position, with the obligation to render an account every year to the aforesaid Superior;
b) future needs with common prudence;
c) the payment of an annual sum for the works of the Order.

Article 77
Permission for Extraordinary Expenses
According to circumstances, the Professed must obtain prior explicit permission from the Superior for extraordinary expenses.

Article 78
Donations to the Order or other Charitable Causes
After having provided for ordinary and extraordinary expenses, the Professed is obliged, with the consent of the Superiors of the Order, to distribute any excess to the works of the Order or to other charitable causes.

Article 79
The Spirit of the Vow of Poverty
According to the evangelical spirit of poverty, the Professed, although living in the world, must limit his requirements, appropriately depriving himself not only of what is superfluous but also of that which is not truly necessary.

Article 80
Effects of the Perpetual Vow of Poverty
With the perpetual vow of poverty, the Professed renounces not only the use and usufruct of his goods but also their ownership and the capacity to possess or acquire temporal goods.

Article 81
Renunciation of Goods before Perpetual Profession
During the sixty days preceding perpetual profession, the Professed in Perpetual Vows must renounce all goods to which he has title in favour of whomever he wishes. This act is subject to actually making perpetual profession.

Article 82
Goods Acquired by Professed in Perpetual Vows
Goods which come to the Professed in any way whatsoever after perpetual profession become the property of the competent Grand Priory or Priory, or of the Common Treasure in the case of Professed *in gremio religionis*.

Article 83
Request for an Indult regarding the Perpetual Vow of Poverty
When fowarding the request to the Holy See for admission to perpetual profession, the Grand Master, with the consent of the majority of the Professed Knights of the Sovereign Council. may for just reasons also request on behalf of the candidate the concession of a special provision concerning the observance of the vow of poverty.

Article 84
Acts subsequent to Perpetual Profession
As soon as perpetual profession has been made, the Professed must take the actions necessary to ensure that its effects are recognized in civil law.

CHAPTER III
Obligations of the Professed in General

Article 85
Duties of the Professed
The Professed, mindful of their high vocation and of the obligations they have freely assumed before the Church and the Order, must conform their lives to the spirit of the Gospel, according to the Constitution and the Code, and strive toward religious perfection.

Article 86
Religious Practices of the Professed
The Professed must fulfil diligently the common duties of the Christian life and, unless legitimately impeded:
a) dedicate at least one hour a day to pious practices;
b) frequent assiduously Holy Communion and the sacrament of penance according to the advice of their spiritual directors;
c) take part each year in a course of spiritual exercises of at least five full days in a religious house.

Article 87
Liberal Professions and Public Offices
Professed Knights may, with the approval of the Superior, practice a liberal profession and accept public office.

Article 88
Regulations for the Activity of the Professed
In conformity with the Code, the Grand Master, with the consent of the majority of the Professed members of the Sovereign Council, is to establish an appropriate regulation regarding how the Professed should dedicate their lives to the apostolate and activities of the Order.

Article 89
Rights of Professed Knights
Professed Knights have a voice in the Chapter to which they belong.

CHAPTER IV
Transfer to another Institute or Society
Departure & Dismissal from the Order

Article 90

Transfer to another Religious Institute

For the transfer of a Professed member of the Order to another religious institute, the norms of Canon Law must be observed.

Article 91

Secularization and Departure from the Order

For secularization and departure from the Order of the Professed in Temporary Vows, the norms of the Code of Canon Law are to be applied, without prejudice to the dispositions of can. 688.

Article 92

Exclusion from Financial Claims of Those who leave the Order

Those who leave the Order can not make any claim against the Order for services rendered or for future considerations. Indeed, before making profession, and after having obtained independent legal advice, the candidate must first sign a declaration to this effect.

Article 93

Dismissal from the Order

Dismissal of Professed from the Order is regulated by the norms of Canon Law.

CHAPTER V
Members of the Second Class

First Section
Knights and Dames in Obedience

Article 94

Promise and obligations

Par. 1 — According to their state in life and in conformity with their own vocation and the directives of their Legitimate Superiors, Knights and Dames in Obedience oblige themselves by a special promise, which binds in conscience, to a life leading to Christian perfection in the spirit of the Order and in the sphere of its works. Conscious of the spiritual value of such a commitment before God, they must diligently observe the divine law and the precepts of the Church so as to be a constant example of piety and virtue, of apostolic zeal and of devotion to the holy Church.

Par. 2 — Knights and Dames in Obedience undertake to utilize their temporal goods according to the spirit of the Gospel.

Par. 3 — Knights and Dames in Obedience do not enjoy privileges or precedence with respect to other members of the Order.

Article 95
Requirements for Admission of Knights and Dames in Obedience
To comply with the requirements for admission the aspirant to Knight or Dame in Obedience must provide proof:
a) of professing the Catholic religion;
b) of not being subject to any canonical or moral impediment;
c) of having completed twenty-five years of age;
d) of belonging to the Order for at least one year;
e) of having the written consent of the spouse, if marriage has been contracted.

Article 96
Procedure for Admission
Par. 1 — A member of the Order who wishes to be admitted to the Promise must submit a written request to the Prior or the Regent and to the President of the Association to which the member belongs together with the documents specified in Art. 95.

Par. 2 — The authority indicated in Par. 1, having heard the opinion of the respective Chapter or Council, proposes to the Grand Master the admission of the candidate to the year of preparation .

Par. 3 — Admission is granted by the Grand Master, with the deliberative vote of the Sovereign Council and the *nihil obstat* of the Prelate.

Article 97
Preparation of Candidates
Par. 1 — The preparation must be carried out under the guidance of a Professed Knight or, in his absence, of a Knight or Dame in Obedience of proven zeal and guidance or by a priest, preferably a Chaplain of the Order, designated by the respective Superior with the agreement of the Grand Master.

Par. 2 —The candidate is to begin and conclude the period of preparation with a course of spiritual exercises of at least five full days in an approved place.

Par. 3 — During the period of preparation, the Knight or priest to whom the guidance of the candidate has been entrusted must take care that the candidate learn about the regulations, history and traditions of the Order. He must form and initiate

the candidate in pious practices, in the exercise of the apostolate and in all obligations proper to the Promise.
To this end, the candidate must practice charity in visiting the sick and the poor, if possible within the framework of the Order's works.

Article 98
Report on the Candidate
At the end of the year of preparation, the person charged with the spiritual guidance is to present to the competent Superior a report on the conduct of the candidate.

Article 99
Admission of the Candidates to the Promise
At the end of the year of preparation, with the agreement of the respective Chapter or Council, the Superior presents the proposal for admission to the Promise for acceptance by the Grand Master, after having heard the Sovereign Council and the Prelate.

Article 100
Promise and Related Acts
Par. 1 — The Aspirant admitted to the Promise pronounces the following formula:
"I, N.N , calling on the name of God, promise faithfully to observe the laws of the Sovereign Military Hospitaller Order of St. John of Jerusalem, of Rhodes and of Malta, to carry out the duties proper to Knights and Dames in Obedience and to render due obedience to whichever Superior shall be given to me.
So help me God, the Immaculate Virgin, Saint John the Baptist our Glorious Patron, Blessed Fra Gerard our holy founder, and all the Saints of the Order".
Par. 2 — The Promise must be received by the Grand Master, Prior or Regent or by his special delegate, in the presence of two witnesses.
Par. 3 — The document attesting to the Promise is to be signed by the Knight or Dame who has made the Promise, by the person who has received the Promise and by two witnesses.
Par. 4 — The original document is to be kept in the archives of the Grand Magistery and a certified copy in the archives of the Priory, Subpriory or Association.
Par. 5 — The ritual of the Promise is regulated by the Ceremonial.

Article 101
Spiritual Duties
The Knight or Dame in Obedience should:
a) collaborate with their fellow members in prayer and works and to this end is bound to recite daily the *Credo* and one *Pater, Ave* and *Gloria.*

b) attend Holy Mass frequently and diligently approach the Sacraments of Penance and the Eucharist according to the advice of their own spiritual director and participate in parochial life;

c) take part each year in a course of spiritual exercises of at least three full days in an approved place, and take part in courses and meetings for formation and instruction called by the Superiors;

d) follow the spiritual rule of life approved by the Grand Master, with the consent of the Sovereign Council.

Article 102
Criteria for Assignment of Duties
In the assignment of duties to a Knight or Dame in Obedience, Superiors must take into account the obligations of their state in life, their abilities, their special professional training and their availability.

Article 103
Change of Tasks
A Knight or Dame in Obedience who, for just cause, has difficulty in fulfilling a prescribed task, should notify the competent Superior who is to assign another activity.

Article 104
Withdrawal from the Promise
Par. 1—The Knight or Dame in Obedience may withdraw from the Promise for important personal reasons.

The request must be presented to the appropriate Superior who will forward it to the Grand Master together with his opinion and that of the respective Chaplain.

The Grand Master, with the consent of the Sovereign Council, is to decide upon the request.

Par. 2 — Upon notification of the dispensation from the Promise, a Knight or Dame in Obedience ceases to be part of the Second Class and returns to original rank. If the dispensation is denied, the Knight or Dame may remain in the Second Class or withdraw from membership in the Order.

Article 105
Disciplinary Sanctions
Culpable failure to observe the obligations which derive from the Promise incurs the application of the disciplinary sanctions specified in Art. 120 and following.

Article 106
Use of the Habit and Insignia
The use of the habit and insignia by Knights and Dames in Obedience is specified and fixed by the Ceremonial.

Article 107
Passage to Religious Profession
Par.1 —The norms of Title II, Chapter I apply to a Knight in Obedience who asks to be admitted to religious profession in the Order and is canonically free to do so.
Par. 2 — The favourable outcome of the process indicated in Par. 1 enables the Knight to commence the Novitiate immediately.

Second Section
Common Requirements

Article 108
Admission of Members of the Third Class
Par. 1 — For admission to the Order, the candidate must be proposed to the Grand Master either by a member of the Sovereign Council with the consent of the Prior or the President of the Association, through the Chancery of the Grand Magistery, or by the Prior or the President of the Association.
Par. 2 — Presentation of nobiliary proofs does not constitute in itself a right to be admitted to the Order.

Article 109
Preparatory year
The reception of Knights, Donats and Dames must be preceded by a preparatory period of one year during which the candidate becomes acquainted with the history of the Order and participates in its works and programmes. The Sovereign Council has the power to dispense from this requirement in individual cases.

Article 110
Reception of Priests
Par. 1 — The favorable opinion of the Prelate is required for the admission of Conventual Chaplains *ad honorem* or Magistral Chaplains.
Par. 2 — The favourable opinion of the *Cardinalis Patronus,* with the advice of the Prelate, is required for the admission of Grand Cross Conventual Chaplains *ad honorem.*

Par. 3 — With the advice of the Sovereign Council, the Grand Master may receive or promote a Cardinal of the Holy Roman Catholic Church to the rank of Bailiff Grand Cross of Honour and Devotion.

Article 111
Holders of Awards
Those decorated with the Order *Pro Merito Melitensi* do not become thereby member of the Order.

Article 112
Nobiliary Requisites
The nobiliary requisites for those who aspire to be received into the Order must be examined on the basis of a special regulation which will be issued by the Grand Master, with the advice of the Sovereign Council, within one year after this Code becomes effective.

Article 113
Requirements for Admission
Par. 1 — To comply with the requirements for admission, the aspirant Knight or Dame must provide proof of profession of the Catholic religion.
Par. 2 — The request for admission, signed by the candidate, must be supported by the following additional documents:
a) a certificate of baptism, a birth certificate which proves age of majority, and a certificate of family status;
b) special titles of merit either received or expected;
c) a letter of recommendation from the proper Ordinary regarding the candidate's life and conduct;
d) a certificate of completion of the preparatory year.
Par. 3 — For priests, it is sufficient to present a letter of recommendation or *nihil obstat* from the proper Ordinary or the Superior of his Order and a certificate of ordination.

Article 114
Admission
Admission to the Order pertains to the Grand Master, with the consent of the Sovereign Council.

Article 115

Admission motu proprio

Par. 1 — The Sovereign Council, the Prior and the President of the Association concerned are to be informed in advance of an admission to be made on the Grand Master's authority alone (*motu proprio*).

Par. 2 — The number of admissions *motu proprio* is determined by the Chapter General.

Article 116

Duties

In accordance with the Constitution, members of the Third Class shall conduct themselves so as to give Christian example in their private and public lives, thus putting into effect the tradition of the Order. It is especially incumbent on them in a special way to collaborate effectively in its hospitaler and social works.

Article 117

Collaboration between Professed Conventual Chaplains
and Chaplains of the Third Class

Chaplains belonging to the Third Class are to collaborate as far as possible with Professed Conventual Chaplains in compliance with the directives of competent Superiors and of the Prelate of the Order.

Article 118

Ceremony of Reception

The reception of members of the Order is to take place during Mass in accordance with the Ceremonial. The presentation of the decree may be made after the rite.

CHAPTER VI
Disciplinary provisions
for Members of the Second and Third Class

Article 119

Disciplinary Sanctions

Members belonging to the Second and Third Class whose conduct is less than exemplary are subject to the disciplinary sanctions provided in the present Chapter.

Article 120
Forms of Disciplinary Sanctions
According to the seriousness of the offence, disciplinary sanctions take the form of:
a) warning;
b) reprimand;
c) suspension;
d) dismissal

Article 121
Warning and Reprimand
No special procedure is necessary for the warning and the reprimand, however it is the duty of the Superior, in the spirit of the Gospel, to correct or remind the member of his duty.

Article 122
Disciplinary Commission
For investigations regarding a suspension or dismissal, a permanent Disciplinary Commission, consisting of three members and assisted by a secretary, is to be constituted in each Priory, Subpriory and Association.

Article 123
Suspension and Dismissal
Par. 1 — Suspension is a temporary disciplinary measure which may be imposed on a member of the Order:
a) if the member is found to be in an unworthy status;
b) if the member has not paid the prescribed contribution for at least two years, and until the position has been clarified and payment has been made of the overdue amount.
Before the suspension, the member's Superior may suggest as a precaution that he withdraw.
c) if the member is under investigation by the courts for grave acts of a moral nature, verified by the Grand Master with the assistance of the Sovereign Council.
In the case of holders of elective offices, the consent of the Sovereign Council, expressed with a two-thirds majority and the vote of the Grand Master, is required. In the case of acts regarding the Order, suspension will not be proposed but internal disciplinary norms are to be applied.
Par. 2 — Dismissal is a defmitive disciplinary measure which may be imposed if a member of the Order:
a) adopts conduct gravely incompatible with the standards of the Order;
b) has not made payment of overdue contributions and persists for another two years in this state of default.

Par. 3 — The disciplinary measures will be imposed by the Grand Master, with the advice of the Sovereign Council, on request of the member's Superior.

Article 124
Preliminaries to Disciplinary Procedures
Par. 1 — The initiation of a disciplinary procedure pertains to the Superior who must communicate this fact to the Chancery of the Grand Magistery.
Par. 2 — The Grand Master with the advice of the Sovereign Council may, for just cause, call the case to himself, setting up a special disciplinary commission.
Par. 3 — As a precautionary measure in every case, the Grand Master has the power to suspend one who is subject to disciplinary procedure.

Article 125
Disciplinary Procedure
Par. 1 — One who is subject to disciplinary procedure must be informed immediately and enabled to prepare his defence within the established period which must be adequate.
Par. 2 — At the end of the established period, the President of the Commission summons the accused before the Disciplinary Commission within a period of not less than fifteen days. During this period, the accused may exercise his right of challenge in accordance with the Code of civil procedure.
Par. 3 —The accused may choose a Counsel, who must be a member of the Bar (or otherwise enrolled as a member of the legal profession in his country with the right of audience in its superior courts) for at least ten years.

Article 126
The Disciplinary Procedure
Par. 1 — Witnesses must be sworn prior to giving evidence.
Par. 2 — Under pain of nullity, the only documentation usable by the Commission is that contained in the acts of the case.
Par. 3 — The discussions are not public.
Par. 4 — Absolute confidentially must be maintained.
Par. 5 — The minutes of the hearing are drawn up by the secretary who signs them along with the President.

Article 127
Disciplinary Resolution
Par. 1 — At the conclusion of the enquiry, the Commission remts the file of the proceedings to the Superior together with a report on the findings of the enquiry.

Par. 2 — Where the findings of the enquiry merit suspension or dismissal, the Superior sends the file and the report of the Commission to the Grand Master to whom it pertains to make the decision, with the consent of the Sovereign Council.

Article 128
Notification of Resolution
Par. 1 — Notification of the disciplinary resolution is conveyed in writing by registered delivery.
Par. 2 — An official record of the notification having been made must be kept in the Magistral Archives.

Article 129
Appeal
Par. 1 — Within thirty days of notification, a documented appeal in writing to the Magistral Courts is permitted against the disciplinary resolutions.
Par. 2 — The appeal may be sent by registered mail with a notice of receipt which attests in such a case to the date of dispatch.

CHAPTER VII
Grades and Honours

Article 130
Grades of the Order
Par. 1 — The members mentioned in Art. 8 of the Constitution belonging to the First and Second Class, as well as the catorgies a), c) and e) of the Third Class, are divided into the grades of:
a) Knight or Dame;
b) Knight Grand Cross or Dame Grand Cross.
Par. 2 — The dignity of Bailiff may be conferred on Knights Grand Cross of Justice and on Knights Grand Cross of Honour and Devotion of the Second Class and Third Class as well as on Cardinals of the Holy Roman Church.
Par. 3 — The honour of the Sash may be conferred on Knights Grand Cross of Grace and Devotion, and on Knights Grand Cross of Magistral Grace.
Par. 4 — The grade of Chaplain Grand Cross may be conferred on Professed Chaplains and on Conventual Chaplains *ad honorem.*
Par. 5 — The form of the insignia of the different classes and ranks is established by regulations approved by the Grand Master with the consent of the Sovereign Council.

Article 131

The Benefits of Commander

The benefits of Commander belong by right:

a) to Professed Knights in Perpetual Vows who have been invested by the competent Priory with a Commandery of Justice;

b) according to the terms of the foundation, to the Knights of Honour and Devotion who are titulars of hereditary *ius patronatus* Commanderies.

Article 132

Honours of the Order

Par. 1 — Upon those who have acquired special merit may be conferred:

a) the Collar *Pro Merito Melitensi;*

b) the Cross *Pro Merito Melitensi;*

c) the Medal *Pro Merito Melitensi.*

Par. 2 — The grade and division, civil or military, of the decoration are regulated by a special statute issued by the Grand Master, with the advice of the Sovereign Council.

Article 133

Requirements for Candidates for Honours

Candidates for honours must be persons of exemplary integrity.

Title III
THE GOVERNMENT

CHAPTER I
The Grand Master

Article 134

Duties

The Grand Master, as religious Superior and Sovereign, is to devote himself entirely to the growth of the Order's works and serve as an example in religious observance to all members.

Article 135

Incompatibility of the Office with Other Positions

Par. 1 — At the moment of acceptance of the election to Grand Master, all offices and prerogatives with which he had previously been invested in the Order become vacant.

Par. 2 — The Grand Master must immediately give up all other activities incompatible with his position.

Article 136

Residence

The residence of the Grand Master is at the seat of the Order, from which he may be absent only for official duties, unavoidable necessity, or for justifiable reason.

Article 137

Authority

The personal authority of the Grand Master extends to all persons, organizations and properties of the Order, in accordance with its laws.

Article 138

Supervisory Responsibilities

It is the duty of the Grand Master to supervise the Conventual houses and churches of the Order, so that proper discipline is observed and religious spirit is maintained, as well as to supervise the institutions authorized to use the Order's emblem.

Article 139

Visitations to the Institutions of the Order

At least once every five years, either personally or through members of the First or Second Class, the Grand Master is obliged to visit the Priories and Subpriories, as well as the Associations and works of the Order.

Article 140

Publication of Documents

In addition to documents relating to his Government, the Grand Master is to ensure that documents of the Holy See regarding the Order are published in the *Bollettino Ufficiale.*

Article 141

Resignation from Office

The Grand Master who resigns from office assumes during his lifetime the dignity of titular Bailiff Grand Prior and is subject only to the Head of the Order.

CHAPTER II
Extraordinary Government

Article 142
Government of the Order during Vacancy of the Office of Grand Master
In all cases when the Order cannot be governed by a Grand Master, a Lieutenant *ad interim* replaces him.

CHAPTER III
The Lieutenant *ad interim*

Article 143
Duties
The Lieutenant *ad interim* shall inform the Holy Father, the Heads of States with whom the Order maintains diplomatic relations, and the various organizations of the Order, of the vacancy of the office of Grand Master.

Article 144
Powers
Par. 1 — The Lieutenant *ad interim* with the Sovereign Council must restrict themselves to the ordinary administration, refraining from initatives that are not necessary or urgent.
Par. 2 — During the period of interim government, the admission of members and the conferment of honours are suspended.

Article 145
Convocation of the Council Complete of State
The Lieutenant *ad interim*, having heard the Sovereign Council, summons the Council Complete of State not earlier than fifteen days nor later than three months from the date of the notification mentioned in Art. 143.

CHAPTER IV
The Lieutenant of the Grand Master

Article 146
Powers

The Lieutenant of the Grand Master enjoys the same powers as the Grand Master with the exception of the prerogatives of honour pertaining to a sovereign.

CHAPTER V
Conferment of Offices and Incompatibilities

Article 147
Conferment of Offices of the Order

Offices of the Order are conferred exclusively upon its members. Exceptions are possible for diplomatic representatives.

Article 148
Incompatibility of Offices

Par. 1 — The same person may not hold more than one of the following offices:
— Member of the Sovereign Council;
— Member of the Government Council;
— Prior, Regent;
— Lieutenant of the Prior;
— Procurator;
— Vicar;
— President of a National Association;
— Member of the Board of Auditors, of the Juridical Council, and of the Magistral Courts;
— Advocate-General.

Par. 2 — It is possible, however, to be a judge of the Magistral Courts and a member of the Juridical Council contemporaneously.

CHAPTER VI
High Offices of the Grand Magistery

Article 149
The Grand Commander
Par. 1 — In the case of the death, resignation from office or permanent incapacity of the Grand Master, the Grand Commander shall exercise the function of Lieutenant *ad interim.*
Par. 2 — In case the incapacity of the Grand Master proves permanent, the Grand Commander must immediately convene the Sovereign Council to deal with the matter in accordance with in Art. 17, par. 2 of the Constitution.

Article 150
Duties of the Grand Commander
Par. 1 — The Grand Commander:
a) assists the Grand Master in fulfilling the charisms of the Order and in the diffusion and protection of the faith, in the supervision of the Priories and Subpriories, and in the supervision of the members of the First and Second Class;
b) compiles visitational reports and the report to be sent to the Holy See on the state and life of the Order.
Par. 2 — Care of the chapel of the Magistral Palace and the organization of pilgrimages of the Order are included in the responsibilities of the Grand Commander.
Par. 3 — The Grand Commander exercises the function of Superior regarding members of the First and Second Class *in gremio religionis.*

Article 151
The Grand Chancellor
Par. 1 — The Grand Chancellor is head of the Chancery and its related offices.
Par. 2 — He is responsible for foreign affairs, the Associations and matters concerning members of the Third Class. To this end he may be assisted by one or more Secretaries-General.
Par. 3 — At the request of the Grand Chancellor, Secretaries-General are appointed by the Grand Master, with the consent of the Sovereign Council. Their appointment is limited to the duration of the Grand Chancellor's tenure in office.

Article 152
Duties of the Grand Chancellor
Par. 1 — The following pertain to the Grand Chancellor:
a) active and passive representation of the Order with third parties;

b) the conduct of policy and the internal administration of the Order, without prejudice to the competencies of the other High Officers;

c) the preparation and despatch of the acts of government as well as the organization of various offices according to the directives of the Grand Master;

d) the arrangement, examination and presentation of subjects to be treated in the Sovereign Council as previously established with the Grand Master.

Par. 2 — The Grand Chancellor supervises the editing of the minutes of the meetings of the Sovereign Council and provides for the drafting of the relevant decisions. The minutes must be approved and signed at the next meeting of the Sovereign Council.

Article 153

Execution of the Decrees of the Grand Master

The decrees of the Grand Master, whether magistral or conciliar, do not have effect if they are not countersigned by the Grand Chancellor.

Article 154

Diplomatic Missions of the Order

Par. 1 — Diplomatic representations are under the direction of the Grand Chancellor.

Par. 2 — The chiefs of mission of the Order represent the Grand Master to the governments to which they are accredited. Even when there are organizations of the Order in the respective countries, it is their responsibility to deal independently with matters as they have been instructed by the Grand Magistry.

Par. 3 — Each individual chief of mission is to submit a report to the Grand Chancellor at least twice yearly or as often as requested by the Grand Chancellor on the political and religious situation in the country to which he is accredited, and on the activities of the Order and its acceptance in the opinion of the public, the local bishops and other ecciesial structures.

Par. 4 — The chief of mission will maintain good and friendly relations with the organizations of the Order in the State in which he works.

Par. 5 — Having heard the Sovereign Council, appointment and recall of diplomatic representatives pertain to the Grand Master, on the recommendation of the Grand Chancellor.

Par. 6 — Appointments of diplomatic representatives of the Order expire after four years and may be renewed for additional four-year terms.

Article 155

Duties of the Grand Hospitaller

Par. 1 — The Grand Hospitaller promotes, co-ordinates and supervises the works of the Priories, the Associations and other organizations of the Order in accordance with the dispositions of the Code, regulations and respective statutes. He inspects the proper functioning of all charitable works which are directly under the Grand Magistery.

Par. 2 — The Grand Hospitaller has the resposibility to ensure that the pastoral directives of the Prelate of the Order are carried out by those who serve in the charitable works of the Order and those who are aided in its institutions.

Par. 3 — The Grand Hospitaller may be assisted in his duties, when he considers it opportune, by a council composed of members who are representative of the different geographical areas in which the Order is present. The members are appointed by magistral decree on recommendation of the Grand Hospitaller and remain in office until the expiry of his mandate.

Article 156
Duties of the Receiver of the Common Treasure
Par. 1 — The Receiver of the Common Treasure:

a) directs the administration of the goods of the Order in co-ordination with the Grand Chancellor, under the authority of the Grand Master and the surveillance of the Board of Auditors;

b) is responsible for drawing up the annual accounts, budgeted and actual, relating to the economic and financial state of the Order, submitting them to the Board of Auditors and to the Grand Master for approval with the advice of the Sovereign Council;

c) is to submit to the Grand Master for approval, with the advice of the Sovereign Council, the acceptance of inheritances, bequests and donations, and the disposal and subsequent reinvestment of the goods of the Order;

d) manages and supervises the Magistral Postal Service;

e) directs and supervises, through of a Secretary General, the internal services of the Magistral household, in particular the Office of Personnel of the Grand Magistery, the Office of Technical Services and the superintendance of the Magistral Palace and other buildings.

Par. 2 — At the recommendation of the Receiver of the Common Treasure, the Secretary-General is appointed by the Grand Master, with the consent of the Sovereign Council, for the duration of the Receiver's tenure.

Article 157
Mandate from the Grand Master to the Receiver of the Common Treasury
Par. 1 — With the mandate of the Grand Master, the Receiver of the Common Treasure supervises the administration of the organizations and works of the Order.

Par. 2 — The Receiver of the Common Treasure must countersign acts of disposal or assignment and contracts which involve the property of the Grand Magistery and the Priories.

Article 158
Residence of the Holders of High Offices
The holders of the High Offices are to have a domicile at the seat of the Order.

Article 159
Vacancy in a High Office
In the case of a vacancy of one of the High Offices, the Grand Master, with the deliberative vote of the Sovereign Council, which is to be convened immediately, proceeds to the appointment by co-optation of a successor who shall remain in office until the next Chapter General.

CHAPTER VII
The Prelate and Clergy

Article 160
Duties of the Prelate
The Prelate, in agreement with the Superiors, is to see that the priestly activity of Professed Chaplains, of those *ad honorem* and of Magistral Chaplains as well as of other priests employed in the spiritual service of the Order be effective and productive in accordance with a special rule which he himself has drawn up and first communicated to the Grand Master.

Article 161
Duties of Professed Conventual Chaplains
In virtue of their religious profession, it is the primary duty of Chaplains of the First Class to devote themselves to the spiritual care of the members of the Order and to the apostolate of its works, in accordance with the dispositions of the Superiors.

Article 162
The Ministry of the Chaplains
Professed Chaplains, Chaplains *ad honorem* and Magistral Chaplains are to:
a) conduct sacred functions on the occasion of major religious solemnities and those which are of special importance for the Order;
b) organize advanced courses in religious education, as well as devotional meetings and exercises;
c) ensure that members of the Order are provided with spiritual assistance, particularly in case of illness.

CHAPTER VIII
Sovereign Council

Article 163
Seat
The Sovereign Council normally at the seat of the Order.

Article 164
Assumption of Office
The members of the Sovereign Council assume office by taking the prescribed oath in the presence of the Grand Master.

Article 165
Agenda and Meetings
Par. 1 — The Grand Master is to prepare the agenda and convene the Sovereign Council at least six times a year or when necessary.
Par. 2 — The members of the Sovereign Council can submit questions and proposals to be included in the agenda.
Par. 3 — The Priors, Regents of the Subpriories and Presidents of Associations have the right to present to the Grand Master proposals pertaining to their responsibilities for consideration by the Sovereign Council.
Par. 4 — The Chancery of the Grand Magistery must give the members of the Sovereign Council adequate notice of meetings and the agenda.

Article 166
Conditions for Validity of the Decisions
Decisions of the Sovereign Council are not valid if they are made in the absence of the Grand Master or of his particular delegate or whenever an absolute majority of the members is not present.

Article 167
Replacement of Members
In cases of death, resignation or absence of more than six months of one of the members of the Sovereign Council, the Grand Master is to invite the Sovereign Council to proceed to the election of a replacement in accordance with the provisions of Art. *159.*

Article 168
Special Cases Requiring a Secret Ballot
In addition to cases expressly provided for, the vote of the Sovereign Council must be secret when it deals with the admission of members of the First or Second Class

or questions concerning individual persons or whenever it is requested by a member of the Sovereign Council.

Article 169

Removal from Office

Par. 1 — It is reserved to the Grand Master, with the consent of the Sovereign Council including a two-thirds majority of those voting, having heard the Juridical Council, to remove a member of the Sovereign Council from office for just cause.

Par. 2 — The conciliar decree of removal may be appealed before the Magistral Courts.

CHAPTER IX
Government Council

Article 170

Place of Meetings

The Government Council is convened by the Grand Master who presides in accordance with Art. 21 of the Constitution. It meets at the seat of the Order or at another place determined by the Grand Master, after having heard the Sovereign Council.

Article 171

Assumption of Office

Members of the Government Council assume office by taking the prescribed oath before the Grand Master.

Article 172

Agenda and Meetings

Par. 1 — The Grand Master is to prepare the agenda for the Government Council which must be sent by the Chancery together with notice of the meeting at least six weeks in advance.

Par. 2 — Each member of the Government Council has the right to propose items for inclusion on the agenda. They must be submitted at least three weeks prior to the date established for the meeting.

Article 173

Minutes

Par. 1 — Minutes are to be taken at each meeting and are to be kept at the Grand Magistery.

Par. 2 — At the end of each session and prior to its conclusion, all resolutions are to be read again and entered in the minutes. Approval of each individual resolution requires the consent of the majority of those present.

Par. 3 — An extract of the minutes containing the approved resolutions signed by the Grand Chancellor is to be delivered or sent to all the members by registered mail with return receipt.

Article 174
Obligation of Secrecy

Par. 1 — Discussions and the minutes are to be kept secret, except for approved resolutions.

Par. 2 — Members of the Government Council have access to the minutes in the offices of the Grand Magistery.

CHAPTER X
Chapter General

Article 175
Convocation

In accordance with Art. 22 of the Constitution, the head of the Order convenes and presides over the Chapter General.

Article 176
Delegates of the Organizations of the Order

Par. 1 — The two delegates who represent Priories in accordance with Art. 22, par. 2 f) of the Constitution are elected, in accordance with the prioral statutes, from the members of the Priory by the Chapter, by a majority of those present.

An alternate delegate may be delegated.

Par. 2 — The Knights in the First and Second Class *in gremio religionis* elect in writing two representative Knights in accordance with to Art. 22, par. 2 g) of the Constitution. The two Knigths who receive the greatest numbers of votes are elected. The invitation to participate at the election is to be sent in writing by the Grand Commander.

Par. 3 — The representation of the Subpriories consists of five Regents, elected in a meeting of the Regents. For each delegate an alternate shall be elected. The assembly in which the Regent delegates are elected is chaired by the Regent of the oldest Subpriory who must set the date and place of the meeting and the agenda.

Par. 4 — The representation of Associations consists of fifteen members elected at a meeting of the Presidents. For each delegate an alternate shall be elected. The delegates do not necessarily have to be Presidents of Associations. The meeting in which the representatives of the Associations are selected is chaired by the President of the oldest Association who must set the date and place of the meeting and the agenda.

Article 177
Place and Date of Meeting and Agenda
Par. 1 — The Grand Master, or the Lieutenant, with the consent of the Sovereign Council, sets the place and date of the Chapter General, giving notice at least six months in advance to the constituent bodies.
Within three months of the day of publication, the Priories and Associations are to inform the Grand Master of the names of the delegates and the alternates elected in accordance with Art. 176.
Par. 2 — At least sixty days before the date set for the meeting of the Chapter General, the Grand Master, with the advice of the Sovereign Council, sets the agenda, sending it to the Capitulars along with the relevant documentation.
Par. 3 — Within thirty days of the date of receipt of the agenda, the Capitulars are entitled, even individually, to send to the Grand Master, in writing, proposals of matters to be included in the agenda, accompanied by appropriate documentation and explanatory reports.
Par. 4 — Until sixty days before the opening of the Chapter General, Knights of Justice can submit to the Grand Chancellor proposals to be considered in the Chapter General.

Article 178
Obligation of the Capitulars to Attend
Par. 1 — The Capitulars are obliged to attend personally unless there is a justified impediment recognized as legitimate by the Grand Master.
The alternate replaces the original delegate for the entire duration of the Chapter General.
Par. 2 — In this case, the elected delegates can be substituted by the alternates designated in accordance with Art. 177. The Chancery of the Grand Magistery must be notified of the substitution at least thirty-six hours before the beginning of the Chapter General.

Article 179
Initial Acts
Par. 1 — The Chapter General begins with the celebration of Holy Mass.
Par. 2 — At the first session, after having verified the credentials of each of the members, the Chapter proceeds to the election, by a majority of those present, of the Secretary and the two scrutineers who are to take the customary oath before assuming their duties.
Par. 3 — The Chairman gives his report on the state of the Order.

Par. 4 — The Prelate presents a report on the spiritual state of the Order.

Par. 5 — The Receiver of the Common Treasure presents a report on the use of funds received from the various organizations and members of the Order.

Par. 6 — The Chairman notifies the Chapter of the requests presented by the Priories, Subpriories, Associations and individual members of the Order.

Article 180
Capitular Commissions
Having heard the reports, the Chapter may elect, by a majority of those present, one or more commissions for the examination of questions and for the preparation of observations and proposals for discussion.

Article 181
Consultants
The Grand Master, with the agreement of the Chapter, may ask members of the Order, without the right to vote, to report on questions of special interest.

Article 182
Election of members of the Sovereign Council, of the Government Council
and of the Board of Auditors
Par. 1 — At the end of discussions, the Chapter General is to elect by separate ballot the individual members of the Sovereign Council, the Government Council and the Board of Auditors in accordance with the Constitution.

Par. 2 — If the candidate elect is present, he is to accept the election or reject it immediately.

In case he is not present, the Chairman is to ask him immediately by appropriate means whether he accepts election..

In both cases, however, at the request of the candidate elect, he may be granted a period of thirty-six hours for reflection.

The Chapter General, after refusal by the candidate elect, moves immediately to the election of a new candidate.

Article 183
Annual Contribution and Passage Fee
Par. 1 — The Chapter General sets the annual contribution and the passage fee to be given to the Grand Magistery in accordance with Art. 9, par. 4 of the Constitution. A five year budget on the use of the annual contributions will be submitted to the Chapter by the Receiver of the Common Treasure after heaving heard the Board of Auditors.

Par. 2. — At least half of the Priors and delegates of the Associations present must approve the contribution as set.

Par. 3 — An Association or, where applicable, a Priory or Subpriory, in which a majority of members are in a difficult financial situation, may apply to the Sovereign Council for a special reduction of the contribution and of the passage fee.

Article 184
Approval and Custody of the Minutes
The minutes of sessions, duly signed by the Chairman, the Secretary and the scrutineers, are submitted to the Chapter General for approval at the end of the meeting. The minutes are deposited in the Magistral Archives.

Article 185
Publication of the Decisions of the Chapter General
The decisions of the Chapter General are published in the *Bollettino UffIciale.*

CHAPTER XI
The Council complete of State

Article 186
Convocation
The Council complete of State is convened in accordance with Art. 145.

Article 187
Delegates of the Institutions of the Order
Delegates of the institutions of the Order referred to in Art. 23, par. 2 (f), (g), (h), (i) of the Constitution are to be elected in accordance with Art. 176.

Article 188
Presiding Officer and Secretary
Par. 1 — The sessions of the Council Complete of State are presided by the Lieutenant in office or, in case of his absence, by the Fligh Officer next in order, provided he is Professed, or otherwise by the Professed member of the Sovereign Council senior in vows.
Par. 2 — The Grand Chancellor functions as secretary of the Council Complete of State and is assisted by another member appointed by the presiding officer.
Par. 3 — When the Grand Chancellor is impeded, the Council Complete of State is to elect a secretary from among its members by a majority vote of those present.

Article 189
Initial Acts
The norms of Art. 179, par. 1 and 2 apply.

Article 190
Election of the Grand Master or of the Lieutenant of the Grand Master
The election of the Grand Master or of the Lieutenant of the Grand Master is by se-
cret ballot, according to the provisions of the Order's law.

Article 191
Consent of the Person Elected
The person elected to the office of Grand Master or of Lieutenant of the Grand Master, having been notified of his election, must signify his acceptance or refusal of the
office immediately.

Article 192
Secrecy Regarding the Election
Until the election of the Grand Master or the Lieutenant of the Grand Master has
been communicated to the Holy Father, all who have participated in the Council
Complete of State are bound to maintain secrecy regarding the result of the election
and the proceedings of the Council.

Article 193
Approval and Custody of the Minutes
The minutes of the sessions are to be approved at the end of the meeting and, after
being signed by the Chairman, the secretary, and the scrutineers, are to be kept in
the secret archives of the Grand Magistery.

Article 194
Closing of the Council Complete of State
With the oath taken by the Head of the Order, the Council Complete of State is dis-
solved.

Article 195
Extraordinary Convocation of the Chapter General
An ordinary Chapter General may follow a Council Complete of State whenever the
Grand Master elect or Lieutenant elect considers this appropriate.
The convocation of such a Chapter, called with the sending of the agenda, can take
place after a reduced interval of sixty days.

CHAPTER XII
Voting

Article 196
Ballots and Counting of Votes

Par. 1 — The election of members of the Chapter General, or of the Council Complete of State, or of Priors, Regents and Presidents of Associations, is by secret vote with ballots which must be destroyed immediately after the voting procedure is concluded.

Par. 2 — For all elections an balloting, the required majority in each case is to be calculated according to the number of persons present who are entitled to vote in the given election or ballot.

Par. 3 — Blank or spoiled ballots, as well as abstentions, are counted. If a majority vote, therefore, is required for an election or an approval of a proposal or a decision, the candidate is elected, or the proposal or decision approved, only if the number of votes in favour is higher than the number of votes against, including the blank and spoiled ballots as well as abstentions.

Par. 4 — In case of a tied vote, the balloting is repeated. If a tie results again, the proposal or decision is considered rejected. In the case of elections, the ballot may be repeated until the tie is broken.

Par. 5 — The members of a Priory, Subpriory or Association who do not reside in the territory of their organization may participate in voting according to their respective statutes.

CHAPTER XIII
The Juridical Council

Article 197
Seat, Powers and Meetings

Par. 1 — The Juridical Council meets at the seat of the Order.

Par. 2 — On juridical questions and problems of special importance, the Grand Master, having heard the Sovereign Council, requests the opinion of the Juridical Council, which is to make its report in writing.

Par. 3 — The President or Vice-President and at least three members are required for a valid meeting.

Par. 4 — The activity of the Juridical Council is governed by regulations approved by the Grand Master, with the advice of the Sovereign Council.

Article 198
Rules of Procedure
Par. 1 — Article *rapporteur*, previously appointed by the President, sets forth the case to be examined. After a collective discussion, the Council decides by a majority of those present. In the case of a tie, the vote of the President decides. The President notifies the Grand Master of the opinion.
Par. 2 — It is in the power of the President to invite the Advocate General to the meetings to express a consultative opinion on the question being examined.
Par. 3 — Minutes are to be drawn up of each meeting, which are to be signed by the President and the Secretary and transcribed in a special book.

CHAPTER XIV
Courts and Judicial Regulations

Article 199
Composition and Seat of the Magistral Courts
Par. 1 — The Magistral Courts are of first instance and of appeal and are composed of a President and two judges.
Par. 2 — The courts meet at the seat of the Order.
Par. 3 — The office of the courts is administered by a Clerk.

Article 200
Incompatibility of the same Judge in different Instances
A judge who has heard a case at one level cannot give a judgment on the same case at a second level.

Article 201
Alternate Judges
The senior judge is to take the place of the President if he is impeded. If it is impossible to constitute a college because the President or one or more of the judges is impeded, the President of the Appeal Court is to complete the college with alternate judges for that particular case.

Article 202
The Oath
Before assuming their duties, the judges and the Clerk of the Courts are to take the following oath before the Grand Master: "I swear to carry out faithfully and diligently the duties of my office and to keep the secret of the office".

Article 203
Age Limit
The age limit for judges is seventy-five years completed. Those who are no longer able to carry out their duties because of certified disability may be released from service by a conciliar decree at any time.

CHAPTER XV
Competency of Magistral Courts

Article 204
Jurisdiction of the Magistral Courts
Par. 1 — The Magistral Courts are competent to decide:
a) on appeals against provisions relating to the necessary proofs for aspirants to the various levels of the Order;
b) on appeals filed against conciliar decrees regarding investiture into *ius patronatus* Commanderies;
c) on disputes relating to the administration of *ius patronatus* Commanderies and of foundations;
d) on labour disputes brought by employees of the Order or by the public bodies of the Order;
e) on suits between persons as members of the Order, including, on the written request of parties who likewise belong to the Order, disputes concerning disposition of the parties' free estates;
f) on disputes between the Order and the public bodies of the Order and between the public bodies themselves;
Par. 2 — On the written request of both parties, even if they are not members of the Order, the Court of First Instance can assume the functions of a board of arbiters to settle disputes, according to law or equity, concerning disposition of the parties' free estate. The activities of the Court are to be without charge except for reimbursement of actual expenses. The decision of the arbiters may be appealed before the Magistral Appeal Court for the reasons set forth in Art. 716 et seq. of the Code of Civil Procedure of the Vatican City State, insofar as these are applicable.
Par. 3 — The Magistral Courts, on the written request of States or subjects of international law, can also function as arbitrator in international disputes.

CHAPTER XVI
Procedural Rules

Article 205

Court Procedure

Except for what has been established in the preceding Articles, procedure in the Magistral Courts is regulated by the norms of the Code of Civil Procedure of the Vatican City State.

CHAPTER XVII
Legal Representation of the Order
before the Court of other States

Article 206

Legal Representation of the Order

Par. 1 — Standing to sue or be sued in the courts of any State pertains to:

a) the Grand Chancellor on behalf of the Order;

b) the Grand Priors, Priors, Subpriors and those with title to *ius patronatus* Commanderies on behalf of those entites;

c) the person specified in the statutes or regulations for Associations and other bodies of the Order.

Par. 2 — In cases referred to in par. 1 (b) and (c) above, legal representation also pertains separately to the Grand 'Chancellor.

CHAPTER XVIII
The Office of Attorney General

Article 207

Advocates of the Order

Legal assistance is provided by the Office of Advocate General which is made up of independent members of the legal profession of eminent repute who are experts in law and versed in the traditions and customs of the Order.

Article 208
Composition of the Office of the Advocate General
The Office of Advocate General is composed of the Advocate General and two alternates who are appointed by the Grand Master with the Sovereign Council for a period of three years renewable.

Article 209
Assistance by the Office of the Advocate General
The organizations of the Order should seek the advice and the assistance of the Office of the Advocate General whenever necessary and especially in cases which involve complex legal issues.

CHAPTER XIX
Defence Counsels

Article 210
Admission of Defence Counsels
Defence counsels may be admitted who meet the requirements stipulated in Art. 125, par. 3.

Article 211
Exclusion and Suspension of Defence Counsels
The President of the Appeal Court may exclude or suspend counsels who, in his judgement, have shown serious deficiencies of a moral or juridical nature.

CHAPTER XX
The Goods of the Order

Article 212
Classification of Goods
Goods of the Order also include those held in the name of Priories, Subpriories and all other organizations of the Order endowed with juridical personality.

Article 213
Contributions of the Institutions of the Order
The Grand Master, with the consent of the Sovereign Council, establishes the contributions of the Priories.

Article 214
Extraordinary Administration

Par. 1 — No new or increased expense can be authorized without first guaranteeing the corresponding revenue or without determining the means to meet it.

Par. 2 — For acts of extraordinary administration, the advice of the Board of Auditors must be sought.

Article 215
Payment of the Contribution

Par. 1 — The Priories and Associations are responsible for the payment of the annual contribution from their members as established in Art. 9 par. 4 of the Constitution and Art. 183 of the Code.

Par. 2 — An Association which has not satisfied its debit to the Grand Magistery before the fifteenth of March of the following year cannot propose the reception of new members or the conferral of the Order's decorations, or be represented at meetings of the Chapter General or the Council Complete of State, until its position has been regularized.

CHAPTER XXI
Board of Auditors

Article 216
Duties

The Board of Auditors:

a) supervises financial administration and the audits accounts;

b) oversees income and expenditures;

c) examines balance sheets;

d) carries out inspection of administration;

e) verifies the accounting and cash balances from time to time;

f) supervises the management of the property of the Order and of the *ius patronatus* Commanderies and other bodies of the Order.

g) gives advice on any question of an economic character either on its own initiative or on request;

h) may, from time to time, request from the Grand Magistery trustworthy personnel qualified for the investigations which they are required to make.

Article 217

Meetings and Compensation

Par. 1 — Ordinary meetings of the Board of Auditors are held twice a year and whenever the President considers it necessary. An extraordinary meeting may be held at the request of the Grand Master or the Receiver of the Common Treasure.

Par. 2 — Members of the Board of Auditors are to be reimbursed for expenses.

Article 218

Minutes of Meetings

Minutes of the meetings of the Board of Auditors are to be approved by its members and signed by the President, with copies sent to the Grand Master and the Receiver of the Common Treasure.

Article 219

Report of the President to the Chapter General

The President is to present to the Chapter General a report on the activity of the Board of Auditors. This. report is to contain a precise accounting on the use made of the annual contributions from the members of the Order.

Title IV
ORGANIZATION OF THE ORDER

CHAPTER I
Juridical Persons

Article 220

Juridical Personality of Entities of the Order

Par. 1 — Priories, Subpriories and Associations have juridical personality insofar as they are part of the juridical structure of the Order.

Par. 2 — Other entities, including foundations or Commanderies, may be granted juridical personality by the Grand Master, with the deliberative vote of the Sovereign Council. Such entities are administered either by the Priory or Association where they are located or by the Grand Magistry itself.

Article 221

Acquisition of Juridical Personality in National Law

The public bodies of the Order may, with the authorization of the Grand Master, acquire juridical personality in the country where they are intended to function.

CHAPTER II
Grand Priories and Priories

Article 222
Establishment of Grand Priories and Priories
Par. 1 — Having heard the advice of the organizations of the Order, and with the consent of the Sovereign Council and the approval of the Holy See, the Grand Master may proceed to the canonical establishment of a Priory and the determination of its boundaries.
Par. 2 — At least five Professed Knights are necessary for the constitution a Priory. They must have canonical domicile within the territory of the Priory that is to be established.

Article 223
Approval of the Statutes of Priories
A Priory is to have its own statutes, approved by the Grand Master, with the consent of the Sovereign Council.

Article 224
Appointment of the First Prior and Council
The Grand Master appoints the first Prior and the members of the Council.

Article 225
Duties of the Prior
By his example, the Prior should motivate the practice of the religious virtues and fidelity towards the obligations characteristic of the Order. In addition he must:
a) make known decrees of the Holy See and of the Grand Master and ensure their observance;
b) at least every three years, visit personally or by a delegate, the institutions dependent on the Priory;
c) promote vocations, foster the works of the Order and supervise the efficient running of the Priory.

Article 226
Meetings and Spiritual Exercises of the Priory
Par. 1 — The Prior is to convene the Chapter for a spiritual meeting and to deal with important matters at least four times a year, or at least once a year if an Association exists in the same territory.
Par. 2 — A course of spiritual exercises of at least five full days must be held each year for all members in each Priory. The Prior is to set the date and place for them.

Par. 3 — Where an Association does not exist, a general assembly of all the members is to be convened in conformity with the prioral statutes at least once a year.

Article 227
Administrative Report of the Priories
The Prior, or the Lieutenant, the Vicar, or the Procurator, is to make an annual report of the administration to the Grand Master and Sovereign Council.

CHAPTER III
Subpriories

Article 228
The Chapter
In accordance with its own statutes, the Chapter of a Subpriory is to meet to deal with important matters; it is responsible for the election of the Regent and Councillors in conformity with what is prescribed for Priories.

CHAPTER IV
National Associations

Article 229
Purpose
Under the authority of the Grand Magistery and the sovereign Council, the purpose of the Associations of the Order is to implement the objectives of the Order as set out in Art. 2 of the Constitution.

Article 230
Membership
Par. 1 — All members of the Order belong by right to the Association of the territory where they reside. Members are exempted from this rule who already belong to another Priory or Association at the time of their arrival in the territory.
Par. 2 — One, who proposes to request admission, for justified historical or ethnic reasons, to a Priory, Subpriory or Association outside the territory where he resides, must obtain the *nihil obstat* from his proper Superior.

Article 231

Conditions for Establishment

Par. 1 — A minimum of fifteen members is required to constitute an Association.

Par. 2 — The Grand Master, with the consent of the Sovereign Council, has the power to divide or re-arrange Associations and their territories when this may be required for the proper functioning of the activities of the Order.

A new Association may be established within the same territory at the request of at least thirty members and with the consent the existing Association.

Par. 3 — It pertains to the Grand Master, with the consent of the Sovereign Council including a two-thirds majority of the Professed Knights, to establish an Association in the territory where a Priory exists.

In this case, the use of the entire estate may be enjoyed by the Priory but it is to be administered by the Grand Magistery as trustees.

CHAPTER V
Delegations

Article 232

Establishment of a Delegation

The establishment of a Delegation requires approval of its working rules by the Grand Master, with the consent of the sovereign Council. In exceptional cases, delegations of one Association may exist in the territory of another with the consent of the Association already existing in that territory.

CHAPTER VI
Churches of the Order

Article 233

Churches and Oratories

Superior are to ensure that each organization of the Order has one or more churches or oratories where the members may meet for pious exercises in conformity with its own statutes.

Article 234

Chaplains of Churches and Oratories

Par. 1 — Each church or oratory is to have a chaplain who cares for it and provides religious services there.

Par. 2 — The appointment of chaplains is made at the proposal of the Prelate, in accordance with Canon Law.

Article 235
Canonical Visitation of Churches and Oratories
Canonical visitation of the churches and oratories pertains to the *Cardinalis Patronus*, in accordance with the Code of Canon Law, either personally or through the Prelate or another cleric.

CHAPTER VII
The Works of the Order

Article 236
"Obsequium pauperum"
Par. 1 — In search of a tangible response to the love of Christ, the first members of the Order recognized the Lord and served Him in sick pilgrims in the Holy Land. *Obsequium pauperum* has its origin in the divine compassion with the misery of the world, which obliges the members of the Order to serve Jesus Christ, who is present in the sick.
Par. 2 — With respect to the other purpose of the Order, *tuitio fidei*, the members of the Order, recognizing the image of God in each individual, are especially called upon to become involved in those situations where human life is threatened in its God-given essence and dignity.
Par. 3 — Consequently, the Order is the tangible way for its members to fulfill the supreme commandment of love for God and neighbour, to honour God and sanctify themselves in the imitation of Christ and in communion with the Church.
Par. 4 — The charism of *obsequium pauperum* leads members to encount the Lord in the sick through personal service. All members are, therefore, called on to practise, personally and regularly, the corporal and spiritual works of mercy.

Article 237
The Organization of "obsequium pauperum"
Par. 1 — It is the exclusive competency and obligation of Associations to set up works of charitable and social service in their own areas in which the members of the various classes can personally fulfill the mission to which they have committed themselves. In countries where Priories but no Associations exist, this responsibility is undertaken by the Priories. Having heard the Sovereign Council, the Grand Master may issue other provisions to avoid, as far as possibile, the duplicaton of responsibilities in the same area.

In countries where charitable and social works already exist outside Associations, they will work, within their defined responsibilities, toward establishing a close co-ordination with the Hospitaller of the respective Association.

Par. 2 — Hospitallers of Associations, or of Priories where there are no Associations, are responsible for relief efforts. Hospitallers are to carry out their duties in harmony with the Presidents, or with the Priors and Councillors.

Par. 3 — Relief activities both outside their own area and those arising from agreements between organizations of the Order, are to be undertaken with the approval of the Grand Hospitaller who is responsible for co-ordination, according to Art. 155 Code.

Par. 4 — Those in charge of the works of the Order must send each year a report to the Grand Magistery on the status of their operations.

Par. 5 — The Grand Magistery initiates works only in exceptional cases.

Article 238
International Co-operation
Par. 1 — In view of the international responsibilities of the Order, the international co-operation of national Associations is of particular importance so that special works of the Order may be advanced. All the organizations of the Order are obliged to work together within their capacities.

Par. 2 — The Grand Master, with the consent of the Sovereign Council, may establish juridical persons within the Order for the administration and promotion of international activities.

Article 239
Sub-Organizations of Associations or Priories for the Execution of Works of the Order
Par. 1 — Sub-organizations of Associations or Priories are foundations, relief services, legally independent works of the Order and similar organizations established for the implementation of the Order's works.

Par. 2 — Such sub-organizations may be set up by Associations, or Priories, provided the following requirements are observed in their statutes:

a) The statutes of a sub-organization cannot become effective before they have been approved by the competent entity of the Order. The same applies to any changes to the statutes;

b) The sub-organization must make a report of its activities to the competent entity of the Order;

c) The President (or head) of a sub-organization, who is to be a member of the Order, cannot assume office without the authorization of the competent entity of the Order;

d) A sub-organization can use the insignia of the Order, or the name of the Order, or claim a link with the Order, only with the authorization of the sponsoring entity of the Order, which also has the power to revoke it.

Whenever these minimum requirements cannot be entirely incorporated into the statutes, as a result of national legislation, their observance must be assured by other means according to circumstances.

Par. 3 — The statutes and proposed amendments must be submitted to be the Grand magistery for its information before they become effective.

Par. 4 — Institutions and activities, which Associations or Priories or sub-organizations of the Order merely assist, but do not manage directly or own, may not use the insignia or name of the Order, without the explicit indication that the institution or activity is simply supported by the Order which assumes no responsibility for it.

CHAPTER VIII
Communication

Article 240
Communications Board

Par. 1 — The Communications Board supervises the internal and external communications activities of the Order and assists the Grand Chancellor and the Secretary for Communications in development and implementation of efficient communications programmes.

Par. 2 — The Communications Board is composed of a President and six Councillors, chosen from members of the Order, competent in various sectors of communications, management, public relations and mass media. Selected to assure reasonable geographical representation, the members of the Board are appointed by decree of the Grand Master, with the consent of the Sovereign Council, for a period of two years renewable.

Article 241
Duties and Meetings of the Communications Board

Par. 1 — The Communications Board advises the Grand Magistery on matters concerning the flow of information, relations with the mass media, public relations, emblems and logos, as well as the organization of the Communications Office, including costs and budgets, personnel and equipment.

Par. 2 — An annual report is to be presented to the Grand Master and the Sovereign Council and to the Chairman of the Chapter General when it is convened. A special report on the activities is also to be presented by the President to the Chapter General.

Par. 3 — The Communications Board is to meet at least twice a year or when the President or the Grand Chancellor consider it necessary.

The members are to be reimbursed for expenses.

CHAPTER IX
Emblems

Article 242

The Emblem for Works of the Order

The emblem for hospitaller activities of organizations of the Order consists of the eight pointed white cross on a red shield, in conformity with the il1ustiation contained in the special regulations.

signed / Carlo Marullo di Condojanni   signed / Fra' Andrew Bertie
Grand Chancellor